No-Problem Parenting™

RESOURCES AND STORIES
that create
CONFIDENCE AND CONNECTION

Edited by Romy Faith Ganser

Published by: Action Takers Publishing - www.ActionTakersPublishing.com

Cover Design: Action Takers Publishing

Paperback ISBN: 979-8-9867817-2-3

Kindle ISBN: 979-8-9867817-3-0

Dedications

I dedicate this chapter to Elizabeth, her parents and her siblings. I am grateful for your trust and friendship. Thank you for the fire you lit in me to make it my mission to help other struggling parents and their resistant children.

~Jaci Finneman

I dedicate this chapter to all the mothers struggling to keep up with their babies and life. Those feeling like a failure, overwhelmed, lost, and not knowing what the next steps are. I see you and hear you, because I was (and sometimes still AM) YOU. You can rock this thing called motherhood with grace and ease with a little self-love, support, and consistency!

~ Dr. Christy Matusiak

This book is dedicated to my incredible parents, who have always set the best example through their actions and way of life. Their commitment to each other and their family is unwavering, and I am forever grateful to have been raised in their loving and nurturing home. Mom and Dad, this book is a tribute to your unwavering love and support throughout my life. Thank you for being the best parents I could have ever asked for, and for instilling in me the values and principles that guide me to this day.

~Denise & Victoria Schwendeman

I dedicate this chapter to my three children, Christiana, John and Shaan, the three best teachers a mother could have.

~Elvira Di'Brigit

This chapter is dedicated to Jack, Ryan, Maggie, and Evan, the seeds I watered. How you have grown into strong, vibrant roses. Thank you for the honor and blessing to be your Momma. I love you to the moon and back!

~Julie Kenzler

To My Family.

~Kate Lund

To All Parents Everywhere...but especially to my son, for giving me the title of Mom.

~Kelly Flood

To my son, Noah. Thank you for healing me in ways I never knew I needed.

~Kay Chorna

To my now-husband, the man who started it all, from just an offhand comment in the McDonald's parking lot.
To my father, who continues to foster the drive for answers I still have today.
And to the key player in my formative years of life, who nurtured the desire for difference.
Thank you.

~Kimberly Gawne

This chapter is dedicated to my mother, Doris Winder, the most resilient person I have ever known.

~Mardi Winder-Adams

This chapter is dedicated to my younger angry self. Thanks for giving me so much pain, problems and heartaches that I finally had to figure out how get rid of you.

~Mort Orman, MD

This chapter is dedicated to my wonderful son, the greatest blessing in my life. I love and am so proud of you!

~Rosalind Sedacca

This chapter is dedicated to the cycle of life and all the generations of my family - those who have passed on, those living now, and those yet born.

~Ruthanne Warnick

Dedicated in loving memory of my son, Sean. I will carry on his legacy by helping others. Sean unexpectedly passed from this life on March 15, 2023. Sean loved to dance and sing and was involved in the Special Olympics in basketball skills and ramp bowling. Sean knew everybody and will be remembered for being a friend to the world.

~Teresa Dawn Johnson

I dedicate this chapter to my mother who passed at the age of 43 and was my strength as I went through my childhood experiences. To my son who is so positive and inspiring to me. To my grandchildren who I hope to inspire to live their dreams.

~Vera Thomas

Table of Contents

Introduction

Have you heard the expression "parenting is a crapshoot"?

Merriam-Webster defines a "crapshoot" as something that has an unpredictable outcome. This definition fittingly describes the unpredictable nature of parenting, but does it mean we leave everything to chance? Does this imply that we can do whatever we want with our children without facing any consequences?

Throughout my 30+ years of experience, I have encountered numerous parents who are deeply engaged in their children's lives, possess exceptional skills, and exhibit immense love and motivation. Despite their best efforts, some parents have unfortunately observed their children fall victim to substance abuse, alcohol addiction, homelessness, or violent behavior. On the flip side, I have had the opportunity to work with children who have experienced challenging situations and trauma due to inadequate resources or their parents' disinterest, incompetence, or overbearing behavior. Despite their challenges, many of these children have demonstrated remarkable resilience, achieving incredible accomplishments.

The saying "parenting is a crapshoot" suggests that no matter how much we try or don't try, our kids will inevitably grow up, *and* there will be factors beyond our control. As parents, we provide guidance, nurture, and support while understanding that our children's actions and choices significantly determine their outcomes. Give them wings and let them fly, as the saying goes.

If you are a parent of children with special cognitive or emotional needs, you may find yourself in the position of being their advocate and protector for life. You may have to search for a safe and supportive environment that can provide them with the care they require long term.

No matter your child's needs or how your family is structured, it's important to remember that you don't have to handle all aspects of your child's life on your own. There is help and hope for your family.

Welcome to No-Problem Parenting™. If you have already gone through the first volume of "No-Problem Parenting™: Raising Your Kiddos with More Confidence and Less Fear," you found resources, tips, and tools to build confidence and overcome parenting-related fears. You learned the three-step framework for becoming the confident parent your kids crave you to be and hopefully you've reached out to some of the authors for support on your parenting journey.

Obtaining support should be effortless, but sometimes our feelings of embarrassment, reluctance, or shame can hold us back.

Enter confidence.

Why is confidence in parenting so important?

Believing in yourself can eradicate hesitations and establish a solid foundation for developing trustworthy relationships. Having confidence in your capabilities and character can facilitate raising your kids, as it alleviates the tension between parent and child, promoting safety and dependability. Confidence is crucial in effectively standing up for your children, advocating for their needs, and securing the resources that best fit your family.

This book, filled with valuable insights from top parenting and mental health experts, is designed to boost your confidence in fostering a strong connection with your child(ren). It features resources and inspiring stories from parents and adult children who have triumphed over challenges. They have achieved intentional yet imperfect parenting, placing importance on advocacy and connection.

Our fundamental belief is in the power of communities, and our ultimate goal is to support parents worldwide with the essential tools they need to care for their families. We make it a point to show our support for small and local businesses recognizing that geographical location should not hinder parents from accessing valuable resources that can significantly improve their family life.

We sincerely hope that this book serves as a helpful guide on your parenting journey, boosting your confidence and strengthening your connection with your child(ren). Remember, your parenting skills do not entirely determine your child's future, nor is their success or failure a direct reflection of your efforts or love. As children grow up into teenagers and eventually adults, they gain their own autonomy and may not always make choices that align with their parents' expectations. Ultimately, we are all responsible for our own happiness and success despite how we were parented. Just do your best and remember you don't have to navigate this journey alone.

Hugs and High Fives,

Jaci

Scan the QR code to connect with the authors

CHAPTER 1

You are the Expert of Your Child: I Believe in You

Jaci Finneman

For as long as I can remember, I've had a passion for helping families and children. I knew early on that it was my calling. But the real turning point for me, when I realized my passion might very well become my career, started in 1993 when I met ten-year-old Elizabeth and her family.

I'd been working as a paraprofessional for children with special needs in our local school district while attending college. A parent of a kindergartener with Downs syndrome asked if I would be willing to provide additional after school care for her daughter. I agreed and was hired part-time by a non-profit agency and became a personal care attendant (PCA).

Several months into the PCA job, my supervisor asked if I would be able to take on another client, a ten-year-old who was diagnosed with reactive attachment disorder (RAD). Aside from having a full plate (I was a full-time student, a full-time paraprofessional with the school, a part-time PCA, and a waitress on the weekend), I knew nothing of mental health, especially not RAD, so I declined.

My supervisor was persistent, and a part of me wondered if she knew something about my skill level that I didn't. So, I went to the public library and looked up the diagnosis of RAD on Microfiche (no Google back then). My first thought was, *What the heck? I am so not qualified to support this family. Why would my supervisor even suggest me?* I discovered that on the severe end of the attachment disorder spectrum are kids like Charles Manson. He was in twenty-five foster care homes by the age of ten. Could that be true? If so, I wondered, *how could he possibly develop a conscious that allowed him to believe adults were trustworthy and loving?* I'd heard of the horrific acts of Charles as an adult and could only fearfully imagine what a young Charles must have been like. I was intrigued, curious, and admittedly freaked out. What if the child they wanted me to care for was as unattached and disconnected as Charles? Again, I declined the request to work with the family.

It was my supervisor's fourth phone call, my avid learner attitude, curiosity, and Mrs. Overdo-It desire to help others that eventually caused me to say, "Okay, I'll give it a try."

I spoke with the child's stepmother, heard the desperation in her voice, and became determined to gain the knowledge and skills to help them.

A few days later, I arrived at the family's house, walked onto the wooden porch, and knocked on the door. The stepmom answered and said, "Here she is. Dad and I are going outside for a break. She's all yours." I thought, *Wow! No wonder this kid has problems. These parents are strict and intense!*

I looked at the beautiful young girl, smiling brightly with rosy-red cheeks and a sweaty forehead, and thought she must have just come in from running around in the backyard.

I would later learn that Elizabeth had been having a tantrum for the past two hours, but when she heard my footsteps on the wooden porch, she stopped screaming, pulled herself together, and turned on a smile. Her mom and dad were exhausted and drained from the tantrum and counting down the minutes until I arrived. Their intense greeting was out of desperation for a much-needed break.

You see, Elizabeth *was* a beautiful girl. Her illness wasn't visible on the outside. Her teachers described her as somewhat quiet and very polite. She was a straight-A student. And her parents agreed. She could be charming, and she could turn rage on and off as fast as the light switch on your wall.

Her early life trauma experience, neglect, and break-in attachment from her birth mother caused her to protect herself, believing that she had to be in control of everything and that even loving people would hurt her. Although her birth father was given twice-a-month weekend visitation and gained full custody on her first birthday, the damage was done, and love was not going to be enough for this little girl.

Because of her charm and brilliance, no one believed her parents when they said she was dangerous.

The first few times I met Elizabeth, I had difficulty believing it was true too! She was very polite, and we had good, quiet conversations. I often caught myself wondering more about her seemingly strict parents' behavior than hers. Still, while I couldn't see what her parents saw, I listened to every word they said, every experience they shared, and everything they had tried to help their daughter.

And then, after just two months' time (thirty hours a week in the family's home), Elizabeth's true colors came through. I began to see what her parents had been experiencing for years. She was very troubled, angry, deceptive, and, yes, she was, at times, dangerous.

Elizabeth trusted no one … including me. Despite having several diagnostic assessments that didn't include the RAD diagnosis, seven out of the thirteen assessments found she was, in fact, suffering from reactive attachment disorder, yet the parents' cries for help were questioned and even judged.

I was confused by the professionals' responses, downplaying the child's behaviors, and blaming the parents, and I didn't understand why the parents weren't being heard. Many of the professionals averted the diagnosis altogether. No one wanted to or knew how to help this child and her family.

My determination to help the family pushed me to read every book, listen to experts present on attachment, and ask questions of my college professors to better understand RAD. I was so intrigued and motivated to learn, and for the first time in my life, I was excited about college. Never had I been so eager to get to class. I wasn't a great student, traditionally speaking, and I had to work super hard to get through my courses, but this diagnosis and my experience with the family fired me up and made me excited to learn more.

Unfortunately, my college professors were not as excited and were of little help. A few weeks into a 400-level psychology class during my sophomore year, a professor scolded me for asking a question about what happens when a child doesn't attach. In a room of about one hundred fellow students, he embarrassed and belittled me, and it was the day I decided my investment in education was better spent shadowing therapists and therapeutic parents in states who were supporting these kids and families with success. I didn't need a degree and really had no desire to be a therapist. I just wanted to help families with their real-life day in and day out challenges in their homes. I left college and my full-time paraprofessional job at the school and began working full-time with Elizabeth's family, determined to find the best therapeutic treatment for them, which we did a long year later.

I acquired so much knowledge that year, but *nothing* taught me more than my regular meetings with Elizabeth and her parents. What they needed most was to be heard, acknowledged, accepted, validated, and supported. They were hard-working, dedicated, smart, fun, generous, and very loving people. Elizabeth's parents wanted to learn; they longed for their child to be okay. As a blended family, they were raising several children, had the typical ups and downs that all parents experience, and were managing fine with the other kiddos. It breaks my heart that Elizabeth and her family had to wait so long to be understood and get the support they needed.

In my thirty-plus years and more than fifty thousand hours of experience supporting kids and parents, I have learned something that has become the foundation of my business:

- I will always believe in parents and support your parenting.
- My job is to help you understand the root of the problem and help you help your child.

When Elizabeth's family moved to live closer to the treatment that would help her, one of her previous therapists invited me to apply for a counseling position within her agency. My experience was equal to the required degree, and I accepted the position and became a mental health practitioner. Ten years later, I accepted the role of program/administrative coordinator for more than eighty therapists and counselors.

I learned so much in my twenty years at that agency—counseling kids, supporting the reunification of kiddos who had been removed from their homes due to abuse or neglect, developing early childhood mental health programs, and hiring and supporting our self-managed clinical teams—yet there was a constant tug on my heart to focus on helping the parents to help their kiddos.

The mental health model changed dramatically over the course of my twenty years in the field, and it began to feel like mental health diagnoses were life sentences for kids and families. Needing to diagnose children to receive funding for services bothered me, and even when we could find a diagnosis that "fit" the child, the funding often wasn't enough, and support or education for the parents wasn't billable to the insurance companies.

I knew there had to be another way to help parents and kids.

In November of 2013, because of a goldfinch and a song (Ep. 32 of the No-Problem Parenting Podcast), I started Hello World, LLC. And now I help you, the parent. I teach you how to become the confident leader your kids crave you to be!

Supporting, educating, and empowering you through a model I call No-Problem Parenting™.

No-Problem Parenting™ teaches you how to give your kids' behavior problems only as much attention as the problem deserves and then how to deal with and overcome those problems. You are the expert of your child, and much like the president of a company, you do not need to be the expert in every area of your business to be the expert of your business.

When I met Elizabeth's family, I thought my job was to help Elizabeth. I realized my heart was in helping her parents.

Ten years after I'd last seen Elizabeth and her family, and totally out of the blue, Elizabeth called me to talk. She was all grown up and the mother of a beautiful child. She told me she wished it had been different back then, yet she was grateful for her parents' resilience and that they elicited the help they needed to put a stop to her downward spiral.

She wanted to thank me for supporting her family, especially her mom and dad, all those years ago. Well, I thanked her too, for the fire she lit in me to make it my mission to help other struggling parents and their resistant children.

Parenting is an honor and a challenge. It is not a merry-go-round; it's more of a roller coaster and sometimes a circus. Just because you have the desire in your heart to raise a child and you have all the love and security to provide for a child or multiple children doesn't mean they will decide to or be able to accept you and your leadership.

When your parenting journey derails, when you don't think you're doing a good job, when you feel rejected by your child, and/or if you feel misunderstood by the people you know and the professionals you've confided in, keep going. There are people out there who will see you, who will hear you, and who will lift you up and acknowledge you. You are the expert of your child; you don't have to prove or defend yourself with anger or desperation. Instead, when you are met with judgment or questioned, in the president of your family voice, thank the person for their time and keep searching. You are the expert of your child. I believe in you.

Jaci Finneman

Jaci Finneman is a parent coach & strategist, podcast host, speaker, and author. With over 50,000 hours of experience, her success with parents and children affected by trauma and mental health diagnoses inspired her to broaden her reach and share her 30+ years of experience with parents facing ANY level of resistance and behavior issues in their home, diagnosis or not!

No-Problem Parenting™ teaches parents to:

1) Seek First to Understand—Why is my child behaving the way they are, and why am I responding (or reacting) the way I am?

2) Prepare for the Worst - Preparing for the "worst" behavior helps parents respond versus react.

3) Change the Conversation - Lead with empathy and give your kids conditional praise they can believe in before pouring on unconditional praise.

Become the Confident Leader Your Kids Crave You to Be!

Jaci's down-to-earth, authentic, and relatable personality adds light, hope, and clarity to her clients. She is 1 of 100 first cousins and enjoys all things baseball, hockey - and dirt. Jaci believes dirt matters! Whether she's getting full of dirt on a muddy 4-wheeling trail or helping you to clean up the "dirt" in your relationships, Jaci believes the outcome and experiences are worth the mess!

Connect with Jaci at https://www.noproblemparents.com/.

CHAPTER 2

Creating Connection, Confidence, and Health Out of Chaos: For Our Kids AND Ourselves

Dr. Christy Matusiak

I remember the day I realized I had been struggling with postpartum depression. My first son was nearly two years old.

It was like a daze of sorts—inexplicable and intangible. Unless you've felt it, no one can understand that pain and lack of energy. The loss of confidence and vitality. It's insidious and sneaky. I had no idea it had happened to me.

Being a holistic chiropractic physician, I didn't think it *could* happen to me. After all, I "knew" all the right things to do. But at the time, I wasn't actually *doing them.*

My primary goal is to help parents and children thrive in this life without the use of medications and surgeries. I am eternally grateful that it was with holistic support I was able to pull myself out of that dark hole. And I've helped many others climb out too! In taking care of ourselves, we not only help produce balance in *our own* lives, but we increase our resiliency and strength, allowing us to show up powerfully for the children we are raising!

I use multiple modalities in my office and connecting the emotional/nutritional components to the structure of the body is incredibly powerful. Here are a few things that my patients have said:

"Prior to meeting Dr. M, other doctors had told me I had to live with the pain, and if I didn't stop running, it would keep getting worse. WOW, they were so wrong! When I met Dr. M, the back pain was so prevalent that it was impacting my quality of daily living, strength training, and running. Dr. Christy helped support adrenal and hormonal issues, and her NET work helped clear out childhood emotional stories that were playing a role in my physical health. She helped get to the heart of the pain, which in turn eliminated the pain." ~ Jen Z.

"My youngest son had been having regular headaches that sometimes lasted all day and some behavior challenges, including what felt like depression. He was miserable, and we were miserable. We had been to our pediatrician, a neurologist, and an allergist—all who could find nothing wrong with him. When we met with Dr. M, she did an analysis and then suggested he go off dairy. After one dairy-free day, his headaches were gone, and he was a happy kid." ~ Michelle P.

"My first son was an extremely colic baby. I started removing items from my diet, but it still continued. I stopped nursing, but it still continued. Tried gripe water, bouncing him softly on a yoga ball, massaging him, but nothing was helping. In Dr. Christy's appointment, she took her time to get to know Nathan as a baby and my labor. She then treated him, which included a slight adjustment. We left there unsure if anything worked until Nathan fell asleep for three hours, which he never did prior. We panicked, and I texted Dr Christy, and she was confident and assured me that something was changing in his body. From the next day forward, he was a completely different child!" ~ Kasia D.

Whether an adult or child, I start at the beginning of your story. I listen to your primary complaint and your goal for seeking care. The answers to issues are often much deeper than you may have initially thought. Think of any issue you or your child may be dealing with currently:

- Thyroid or other hormonal imbalances?
- Digestive complaints or colic?
- Sleep problems?
- Recurrent colds, ear infections, or other immune challenges?
- Skin conditions or stubborn rashes?

These seemingly simple issues are often multidimensional. Human beings are spiritual/emotional/energetic beings—having many angles from which we can approach problems in the body. So, I address problems from many perspectives: structurally, nutritionally, and emotionally. In my experience, it is rare that someone experiences a health challenge that is only created from one of the above areas. For instance, think deeply about yourself or your child's health situation, and answer the following:

- Did you have an injury or trigger that seemed to initiate the problem?
- What is your typical diet like on an average day?
- How much water do you drink daily?
- What, if any, supplements/vitamins do you take?
- What stressors are currently impacting you?

Our bodies hold onto every memory, and our cellular makeup keeps track of every event in our lives, no matter if we consciously recall the event or not. Even traumas during a pregnancy (whether real or perceived) can affect not only the mom but also the growing child. Our bodies hold onto these traumas like a resource library, ready to pull from its stacks at any time to build evidence or protect us from pain. Answer some of these questions for yourself, or on behalf of your child, if either of you is struggling to find an answer to a health issue or condition:

- What was your mother's pregnancy like with you? Any stressors that impacted *her* while you were inside of her?
- What were the circumstances around your birth/entry into the world?
- Were you breastfed? And if so, for how long?
- Were there any traumas, emotionally or physically, that impacted you growing up, whether you remember them or not?

I share in my book, *Coordinating the Chaos: Through Birth and Burnout*, my own birth stories of my three boys. If you ever choose to get it—spoiler alert!—I had *very* different birth experiences with each of my kids, and they are mirrored to this day in each of their personalities, and who they are is reflected in how they manifest, deal with, and heal from illness!

My oldest was born in the hospital, after a 44-hour long labor/delivery, where I was exhausted, incredibly emotional, and depleted. He has tendencies toward fear-based thinking and anxiousness, but is an amazing kid that will fight to the death for what he wants or believes in.

My middle was born in the car, in front of our midwife's office, in a very intense, quick delivery, where I was left feeling empowered. He is a little sneaky, strong like an ox, and is the most rambunctious/energetic, requiring lots of outdoor time.

My youngest was born in a planned home birth, in the peace of our bedroom, which, while also intense, allowed for a more relaxing environment and entry into the world. He is the most "type B" personality and very "go with the flow" (which can sometimes be a challenge for myself and my husband)!

Picture the energy created in *my* body and therefore transferred into each of my sons' bodies during each delivery. Again, our bodies remember *everything*. And because of the amazing connection between the mother and the baby, they feel what the mom feels and can absolutely carry some of that energy from their birth experience (and other early life moments) into their lives.

Aside from the energetic component of the birth experience, there are scientific/tangible impacts too. I have some patients who describe their birth experience ending in a C-section, and they report that they were not breastfed. It's almost classic that these individuals often suffer with asthma, frequent colds, skin conditions such as eczema or psoriasis, and digestive imbalances. These scenarios are commonly impacted by dysbiosis—an imbalance of the gut flora that the child missed out on in the early days. Clearly, nutrition and the chemistry of the body and GI tract can have an effect on many aspects of health, including mental.

When working with people experiencing any stressful event, it's important to recognize the potential hurt and insult to the person's body and nervous system as a result of this "trauma." Whether it's the death of a loved one, a divorce, moving, a major health event, or a job loss, the bottom line is that the traumas we experience in our lives, from the second life begins through the present moment, have an impact on who we become and how our bodies can create either health or disease as a result.

Yet here's the thing—shifting all of this is all within our control. We get to rewrite the stories and rebalance our bodies emotionally, nutritionally, and physically with relative ease—if we choose! And the most amazing thing? When we are talking about babies and young children in those first few years, the sooner we focus on our own and our child's healing, the fewer layers and compensations are created, allowing deeper clearing and health.

When babies are balanced physically, energetically, nutritionally, and emotionally, they get sick less often, sleep better, and are less likely to develop behavioral issues or other health conditions as they grow. And even if they do succumb to an infection or problem of some kind, their recovery is faster and easier with less "baggage" holding their nervous system hostage! My kids, to this day (12, 9, and 7 years old), have *never* taken an antibiotic or over-the-counter medication of any kind. This doesn't mean they haven't fallen ill from time to time. I simply look beyond the symptoms and have other tools that have generally provided fast and deeper relief and healing!

There is a system called neuro-emotional technique (NET) that I utilize in my office. It helps you disconnect the stress and past subconscious patterns in your body. Using muscle testing, the practitioner energetically communicates with your nervous system, identifying the emotions and organ systems/meridians that are weak/out of alignment. Through determining the past triggers and patterns and combining them with physical corrections in the body, we literally clear your nervous system of the hold that those emotions have on your body.

While I clearly love the emotional components of one's well-being, I never downplay the importance of other basics when helping babies (or their parents) maintain health—without medications! Eating the right foods/getting the right supplements that are specific to each person is important, as is keeping things in flow structurally. Chiropractic has been around for over a century, and it is incredibly powerful when seeking to help release the body's innate ability to heal from literally anything! Through addressing all dimensions of a child's health, we have conservatively handled ear infections, colic, spit-up, sleep problems, colds/flus and other viruses, rashes (diaper or otherwise), delayed milestones, and more!

I'd like to leave you with a few lists of the best things I think you can do to support your baby's health in that first year or two. And remember, this is not to judge or shame if you made or make different choices, but just reminders to enhance their growing bodies and minds if, and wherever, possible. And if your child is no longer in this stage, extrapolate for the ideal comparison for your child's age and your stage!

Breastfeed, if possible, for as long as is mutually desired between mom and baby.

Snuggle and love on your baby! There is no spoiling a child with attachment and comfort. Look at the animal kingdom, and you'll see that other primates have been attached to their young in this way for years.

Provide them an opportunity for tummy time and freedom of movement. This allows for less restriction and open exploration mentally and physiologically.

When introducing solids, begin with vegetables, proteins, and healthy fats. Save fruit for last, as often, beginning with sugars sets their palate for that desire. I also tend to suggest avoiding dairy products and grains until after 12 months.

Learn about homeopathy to treat simple conditions.

Let a fever run its course (within reason) instead of lowering it with medications. Homeopathy is fantastic to use here.

Moms:

1. Maintain *your* health and energy, as your baby is incredibly sensitive to you.
2. The healthier, and happier, you are, the better off your child will be!
3. I recommend that on a daily basis, moms (and everyone) get adequate quality and quantity of these **7 best doctors**:

- Sunlight
- Fresh air
- Nutritious food
- Water
- Sleep
- Exercise
- Joy

Self-care for moms is a topic near and dear to my heart. I go into detail about each of the seven best doctors in my book, *Coordinating the Chaos—Through Birth and Burnout*. Because, at the end of the day, if you are depleted, you are not there to support the needs of your growing child. Therefore, taking care of yourself energetically, physically, nutritionally, and emotionally is priority #1!!

It is with love and gratitude that I encourage you to keep awareness of your own and your child's health journey! Everything we experience is part of our story, and sometimes just a little reflection can change everything! Best wishes to you and your family.

Dr. Christy Matusiak

Dr. Christy Matusiak is a holistically driven chiropractic physician practicing in Wilmette, IL, with Integrated Holistic Healthcare. She has spent over the last decade helping patients overcome autoimmune conditions, digestive issues, hormonal imbalances, musculoskeletal pain, chronic inflammation, and more. She focuses on identifying the root cause of these conditions by addressing all areas of health (physical, nutritional, emotional, and energetic).

She hosted YouTube channel *Dr. Christy Cares*, where she shared videos with secrets on living a naturally healthy life. She also authored the book *Coordinating the Chaos: Through Birth and Burnout*, supporting the newly post-partum mother through life and helping her create the mental clarity to be present for her growing family. Dr. Christy shares her own experiences and those of patients to guide women through this stage of life with ease! The book also provides holistic tips on maintaining your baby's health! She's currently working on part two of the series, with tips on coordinating the chaos through toddlerhood!

Dr. Christy has been married for over 17 years and is a mom to 3 boys, ages 12, 9, and 7. She remains active with them and is committed to her own health and physical fitness. She recognizes that one's journey toward wellness is always evolving. Through this, she strongly values growth and self-reflection, believing that "health begins within each of us!"

Connect with Dr. Christy at https://linktr.ee/christymatusiakdc.

CHAPTER 3

The Power of Play: How Sports Can Build a Child's Confidence

Denise Policano Schwendeman
and
Victoria Schwendeman

As parents, we all want our children to grow in confidence. Just as we nurture them through the food we feed them, and the education and experiences we provide for them, nurturing self-belief lays the foundation for a confident person. Building confidence requires identifying an individual's strengths and the time to refine that strength to a skill. It's a belief in our abilities and skill set that deepens with practice and experience. A child's self-belief and confidence requires guidance from parents, teachers, coaches, and other influential people in their lives. Playing sports can be a wonderful way to cultivate self-belief and confidence.

I'm writing this chapter together with my daughter, Victoria, because her involvement in sports, from a young age, and the confidence and life skills she learned throughout her sports career, continue to guide her choices in her life today. She is now a coach, herself, to hundreds of children!

Hopefully, our combined thoughts will provide suggestions to keep balance, physically and mentally, in the forefront as you guide your child to build self-confidence through their involvement in sports.

Building confidence through playing sports

Introduce your young children to age-appropriate sports. Town or city organized sports are a great way to get them started. Through sports they will meet new friends, be physically active, feel included in something larger than themselves, learn to play with a team mindset, and start developing skills necessary for sports and life. Beginning as early as ages 4-6, children could start to show an interest in sports, whether that be one sport or many. Introduce them to as many sports as possible to let them explore different activities and have fun with friends. At this age, there should be no pressure, only positive reinforcement and feedback. At ages 6-12, your child might start gravitating towards a specific sport or two. It also seems likely they have begun to comprehend the importance of putting time and hard work into the development of their skills. At this level, the focus should be on encouraging teamwork, as well as developing friendships with teammates, friendships that could last throughout their athletic career and beyond. Many former teammates from Victoria's athletic career have become some of the most important people in her life. This stage is crucial, because a sports career will eventually end, but the connections you make can last a lifetime.

When children reach the ages between 12-18, they could become specialized in one sport and might even start to consider playing that sport at a higher level. Recognizing the importance of setting goals and working towards them in order to achieve sport specific success may start at this age. This is when the child should start to develop time management skills in order to create a healthy balance between their sport and other aspects of life, such as family, friends, and social life. Parents, at this point, you should consider finding good quality coaches, ones who prioritize a growth mindset, so your children learn the importance of practice and perseverance. Not all coaches are created equal, so make sure you look at all the options available to you.

We never know how well our children will do in sports. There are so many factors that can influence a child 's ability to excel in a particular sport, including genetics, training, coaching, and overall health, and wellness. Therefore, it's important to support your child's interests and encourage them to pursue their passion, while also keeping an open mind and being flexible to change as their interests and abilities evolve over time.

Check in:

As you support your child in their chosen sport, check in often to see how they're doing by asking yourself this set of questions:

- Are they having fun?
- Are they developing healthy relationships?
- Are they excited to go to practice?
- Are you and their coach focusing on their strengths?

Nurture Your Young Athlete

Focusing on what they're doing well and building on those strengths will encourage them to continue playing a sport and begin the process of building confidence. So often when we focus on their weaknesses, so does the child and when this happens their confidence can diminish. Focusing on weaknesses creates stress and can turn them off to the sport, just when they've only begun playing.

Keep in mind sports are supposed to be fun, especially at a young age! Get outside and play with them. This time spent with them will keep them active and enhance their love for the sport. When you make it a fun family activity, the sport becomes even more enjoyable. Soon they will begin to relate to you on a different level and the bonding that comes from this will further support their self-belief. This also develops their skills even more through play without putting an emphasis on practice. There's nothing wrong with practicing, but younger children especially will thrive on time spent with their parents just playing. This investment of time will benefit your child many times over throughout their lives.

Keeping the fun in sports

When children are first starting out in a new sport, it should be all about fun! This is the stage where they will make all kinds of positive connections. They will: connect with other children their age who are having fun at camps and clinics; meet coaches who root the foundation of the sport in a happy and healthy learning environment; and lastly, they might just find that spark that drives so many to playing sports at higher and more competitive levels. The important thing for parents to remember is to DO YOUR RESEARCH. As a coach, I know that not all coaches are created equal. Reach out to other parents who have put their children in a specific program to really make sure your child will thrive and develop a healthy mindset in sports.

Now, let's move onto sports at a higher level. Keeping the fun in sports is just as important as your child progresses in their athletic career. Freshman through senior year of high school, I was starting varsity and played for national level travel teams, the top level for my specific sport. It was never a burden, because of the coaches and people that my parents helped to surround me with. At that point in my life, everyone I came into contact with genuinely wanted to be there, wanted to see their players and teammates get better and wanted to put all of our effort into learning as much as we could to attain our common goals, both short and long-term. This changes the game for children when they connect with their teammates and really drive each other towards achieving athletic goals. When this happens, it becomes a collaborative effort leading to individual and team successes. It's fun whether it's day one, or the last game of their athletic career. Finding a space where your child feels safe and supported in their growth is crucial to maintaining their overall happiness and preserving their love of the sport.

Naturally, your next question might be, what can parents do to make sure their child can have a positive experience? As was stated above, do your research! Do not be afraid to ask questions and advocate for your child. The one thing you want to be sure about is doing so in a respectful manner towards coaches and athletic organizations. Set attainable goals, both short and long term. This way, the child is less likely to be disappointed and more likely to learn the importance of setting goals in life beyond sports.

Mental Health in Sports

As a former athlete, now coach, who has played at some of the highest levels, finding a balance between managing the demands of your sport and your mental health is imperative. Today, coaches see less rolled ankles taking players out of their sport and more mental health issues. Rather, it is that the demands of a sport become too much for the athletes to handle mentally and emotionally. I was also a D3 collegiate athlete, and this was the first time in my athletic career that my mental health suffered. I fell completely out of love with playing the sport that was my greatest love, escape, and happy place since sixth grade, and it was devastating. Even though I was at my dream university and had some wonderful teammates, my career in college sports was trying. This is why I am such an advocate for finding a good quality coach because, had I had one, maybe my collegiate experience would have been better. While I fell out of love with playing, I got that love back through coaching. Nothing feels better than seeing a child, whom you coached, achieve their goals, while simultaneously growing as an athlete and a person.

One of the biggest things parents can do is to check in with your child. See if they are still enjoying the sport or if it has become a burden. Yes, coaches do see differences in children if they seem to be having an off day, however we see them maybe a few times a week for a handful of hours. Parents live with their children and see them multiple times throughout a 24-hour period. If you notice something is off, talk to your child and get an understanding of what they're feeling, then talk to the coach to see if something can be changed or corrected to lighten that weight off the child. Each child is different, some may need a week or two off to reset, others may need more time off or even an indefinite leave. Keep in mind that there might be external factors, not the sport, which are affecting the child. An important mindset that I learned early in my career was that your sport should be your escape. For those two hours a day that you are on the court, field, etc., at any age, it can be your escape from other pressures in life.

You get to go play a game with your friends and the game is fun! If your child learns to cope mentally, especially if they choose to pursue a sport at an elite level, then you are helping to set them up with confidence to handle any situation or adversity.

Closing thoughts

Sports are incredible, they have the ability to unite like-minded individuals in something that is bigger than one person. They teach invaluable life-lessons that truly serve former athletes throughout their lives. These tangibles prove why young children should be involved in sports at some point in their childhood or teen years. It might seem cliche, but to quote the incredible soccer star:

Success is no accident. It is hard work, perseverance, learning, studying, sacrificing, and most of all, love of what you are doing or learning to do. ~Pelé

Everything in this quote applies to sports and if children learn this and carry it through life, there is nothing that they cannot accomplish.

Denise and Victoria Schwendeman

Denise Schwendeman is a seasoned expert in the field of essential oils, with over 15 years of experience. As a leader of thousands, she has made significant contributions to the essential oil industry, and currently works with the largest essential oil company in the world.

With a deep passion for health and wellness, Denise has dedicated her career to educating others about the benefits of essential oils - helping them integrate these oils into their daily routines to support optimal health. She is a published author in the Amazon #1 Best Seller, "No-Problem Parenting – Raising Your Kiddos with More Confidence & Less Fear."

Denise is a proud mother of two adult children – both of whom she works with in the business. She values family & friends and cherishes the memories created together. In her free time, she enjoys reading & researching, traveling, and exploring new cultures.

Victoria is an accomplished athlete who started her athletic journey at a young age. Her talent and dedication to volleyball earned her an athletic scholarship to a Division 3 University.

Victoria chose to stay involved in volleyball and give back to the next generation of young athletes. She found her calling in coaching at the high school level, where she works with young women helping them improve their volleyball skills and build confidence in all aspects of their lives both on and off the court.

Connect with Denise at

https://www.doterra.com/US/en/site/deniseschwendeman.

CHAPTER 4

Three Keys to Connecting with Your Daughters to Create That Bond of Deep, Lasting Trust

Elvira DiBrigit

The changes our daughters go through during puberty can be stressful for everyone. How we deal with it as parents can affect the relationship we have with the teens they are becoming.

If you have a daughter in her teen years, I'm guessing you might be where I was about 15 years ago; feeling frustrated because your daughter won't listen and doesn't want to talk to you. She is probably spending all her time in her room, or on her phone. And she probably thinks she knows everything, right?!

Once they start turning inward, we might feel a bit desperate. We realize we are running out of time to pass on our advice, our wisdom.

I am a mother of three children, two of whom are now in their late twenties, and I know how the teen years can sneak up on you. I started making a habit of telling all my friends with 10-year-olds that the end was near!

This may seem extreme, but I would tell them that they seriously needed to prepare for the big changes ahead. Because I frequently hear from parents that their child, around age twelve, suddenly, one day, seems like a totally different person. In fact, researchers at Arizona State University found that the pre-teen years can be the most stressful time for parents.[1]

What I kept seeing as a homeschool teacher and coach, was that many families would quit homeschooling when the children entered the teen years. There are various reasons for this, but primarily it's because the parents didn't know how to deal with what they perceived as attitudes and power struggles.

I mentored a mother whose eleven-year-old daughter was expressing some big emotions. I coached her to help cultivate a trusting, close relationship with her preteen. A couple of years later she told me, "She's thirteen now and moodier. We still talk sometimes, but she spends a lot more time in her room. I get it that peer friendships are vital at this age, but it's still hard for me."

With my own daughter, I saw this shift early because I was waiting for it and knew the early signs. I've worked with children most of my life, studied human development, and became a Waldorf teacher before my oldest turned five years old. Yet, I still had so much to learn about having a tween at home, and I learned a lot from my mistakes.

For example, I remember trying to have one of the "talks" with my daughter on a long car ride. I was uncomfortable with the sex talks, even though I was a young "hip" mom and didn't think I would have this discomfort. I didn't know how to start, and soon she was plugging her ears and singing loudly so my words wouldn't get through. I was worried because I wanted to keep my girl safe, but how could I if she wouldn't listen to me?

Eventually, I figured out how, and I was able to create that deep connection and that trust before she left home. Now, I work to create that reality for other families. I love helping moms connect with and empower their daughters and then seeing them both live their dreams.

I call myself a Puberty Doula. Parents need a puberty doula because it's very challenging to know what to do when your child suddenly undergoes so many changes.

Much of what I'm sharing with you comes from my wish that I had known things sooner and done things differently with my own daughter. I was able to learn new ways, and shared these with others over the years as a homeschool teacher and parent coach. Some of what I share comes from studying non-violent communication and becoming certified as a positive psychology practitioner.

Parents I work with often ask; How can I get her to listen? How can I get her to talk to me? How can I keep her safe in this crazy over-sexualized world we live in? Most parents want to empower their daughter, but don't know how to do so in an age-appropriate way without threatening her innocence.

It's not just hormones and physical changes. Tweens are closing the door to their room because they are like a caterpillar in a cocoon. They are giving birth to a new being. They are going into a dark space, turning into mush. (Their brains sure do seem like mush!)

I'm excited to share how you can create that close relationship with your daughter, where she feels safe to come to you as her confidant. First, you need to know that your daughters want your love and guidance. But they need that guidance in a different way once they get to their teen years.

There are three secrets to mother/daughter bonding that I've found after years of experience and research. I break it down into:

1. Focus on Character Strengths.

2. Teach Feminine Cycle Awareness.

3. Use Storytelling Therapy.

I've been testing these and have had amazing results. One of the moms I worked with found that by just applying the first of these, she saw her daughter become more receptive, more willing to try new things, and even offered to help around the house! Amazing, right!

Key #1: Focus on Your Child's Character Strengths

There are three needs every human has besides air, water, and food. We also need competency, autonomy, and connection. Scientists have found that these three things dramatically impact our sense of well-being. You can help meet these three needs of your child by reminding them of their top character strengths.

Psychologists and social scientists did a huge global survey, and they found that there are 24 universal human character strengths, and we each have a different combination of these, which makes up our personalities. (Find a PDF on my website for more information.)

By knowing how to make the most of character strengths, we can help our child feel competent. Not just *feel* competent, but to actually help them see their own real self-worth.

As parents, there's a natural tendency to focus on what needs to be improved, or fixed, in our children, but this often leaves our children feeling like they aren't enough.

That's a feeling most women I know deal with on the daily. The subconscious belief that they aren't good enough. Even very successful women I know feel this way. We do not want to keep passing this on to the next generation!

When one mom figured out her daughter's strengths and did a few activities that I shared with her, she reported back to me that it was like the difference between giving an empty compliment vs. a real appreciation - her daughter felt the difference.

Then of course, this led to her willingness to talk and to listen. She felt understood, and appreciated for who she is.

By focusing on your child's strengths, you can create a positive basis for connection, which is really the starting point for improving a relationship.

Tip: Everyday, notice and comment on how your daughter is using one of her strengths. This will build positivity between you. It takes practice to make this into a habit. It can't just be an occasional good word here and there.

Key #2: Teach Feminine Cycle Awareness

When I was a teen, I didn't really understand the normal part of my emotional ups and downs. I often thought there was something wrong with me. I didn't know how my hormones affected my inner experience until I was in my late 30s. There's so much lack of education in this realm, because talking about menstruation has been taboo for so long. Even now, with people having period parties or ceremonies for their daughters, those same families might not really understand the four phases of the monthly cycle and how to be empowered by this knowledge.

We must connect to our daughters through our shared experiences. What is the one thing we all share as women? Our cyclical nature. Communicating the wisdom of feminine cycles to our daughters is where our power lies.

Start learning about your menstrual cycle, the internal and external changes from hormones that happen throughout the whole month, not just your bleeding time. Chart these changes together.

Instead of complaining about her hormones and all the drama, we can educate her about those ups and downs, and we can be supportive. You want her to feel she can come to you with all her questions - but are you comfortable when she does? Because if not, you need to work on that.

When we are hiding our menstrual products, or not using the correct terms for body parts, then we are communicating shame. When we just focus on teaching our daughters about periods and pregnancy, we are leaving out a lot of the female experience.

You want to have a daughter who is empowered to make good choices. The way to do this is to have hundreds of little talks, not just a few big talks. Help her see the whole cycle of life from maiden to old woman. *The Heroine's Journey*, as I refer to it in my classes.

We don't have to do this alone. When I took my daughter to women's gatherings, where women were talking about what they were learning at different stages of life, and where life transitions like first periods and menopause were celebrated, it brought us so much closer together as mother and daughter. This is the kind of community I love to create now with my mother-daughter groups.

Key #3: Storytelling

It's an easy pattern to get into, to nag our children to do something and drill them on what not to do. When we do this, we can see our children tuning us out. But telling a story about what might happen to someone who does (or doesn't) do something, gets them listening and thinking.

Humans are wired to learn through storytelling. For hundreds of generations, elders of indigenous cultures around the world have been teaching through storytelling and parables. Often, they don't even share the ending. Instead, they ask the listener, "What would you do in this situation?"

At Princeton University, researchers did a study with storytellers and listeners.[2] They hooked participants up to EKG machines, and when the storyteller got part way into the story, the same part of the brain lit up in the listener as it did with the storyteller! That's neuro-synchronicity; they were connected.

It doesn't even have to be a story from your own experience. You can tell a story by saying, "I read online today about these people who …" Or even better with teens, "I saw a meme today that got me thinking…"

Brene Brown's message about story stewardship is also very powerful for mothers and daughters. When your daughter is telling you her story, don't make it about you by immediately trying to give your opinion, sharing your experience, or trying to make her feel better. Be a good steward by doing some active listening.

I'm sure you already know that rates of teen depression and anxiety have been increasing in recent years, even before Covid. These are the things we can hope to avoid, by creating a healthy bond with our daughters.

If you've read this whole chapter, then you obviously want to build a strong connection with your daughter. You want to empower her to live up to her full potential.

I know we have just barely scratched the surface of these topics. Some of you will be able to take this information and run with it. Some of you may feel overwhelmed. You might be in a rut and need some further guidance. If that's the case, I encourage you to contact me.

As I always say: raising a daughter might be one of the toughest things you do in your life, but it can also be the most rewarding!

1. https://psycnet.apa.org/record/2015-48444-001. (Luthar, S. S., & Ciciolla, L. (2016). What it feels like to be a mother: Variations by children's developmental stages. *Developmental Psychology, 52*(1))
2. https://www.pnas.org/doi/10.1073/pnas.1008662107. Speaker–listener neural coupling underlies successful communication. Greg J. Stephens, Lauren J. Silbert, and Uri Hasson

Elvira DiBrigit

Elvira (El-veera) DiBrigit is known as The Puberty Doula for her work as a parenting coach and teen mentor. She primarily works with moms who feel unprepared to face the challenges as their daughters transition through puberty and adolescence.

Elvira is a credentialed Waldorf teacher, and positive psychology practitioner, who brings over 20 years of experience helping parents connect more meaningfully with their children.

When she is not working online, you can find Elvira swimming in the ocean, or working with her husband and teenage son on the family farm/retreat center in Hawaii.

Connect with Elvira at http://Thepubertydoula.com.

CHAPTER 5

Be In It

Helen Harwood Snell

Who am I to write a book on parenting? I'm not a professional coach. I don't have a career in child services. I'm not even sure I'm a good parent. I'm sure I've made my share of mistakes, but that admission is one of the first steps to no-problem parenting. There will always be problems. It's how to react to them and move through them that changes everything.

We all think we're getting it wrong. You can read the parenting books. You get pamphlets and resources from doctors and parenting groups. You get (mostly) unsolicited advice from friends and family. No matter what you do to prepare, there is nothing like being in it.

That's the heart of it for me. Just be in it. Play at their eye level when they're small. Take an interest in the things they're interested in. Do your best to show up for school events or sports. Do your best, period. Make a mistake and move on. We are going to make mistakes, and I think the sooner we accept that, the less stress we will have. When love is behind your actions, it will show.

None of my brood fit the typical school system here in Ontario, Canada. One was identified as *gifted* and was offered a unique educational approach for several years that benefited her in many ways but, challenged her socially. One was slow to read, so his comprehension suffered, along with his self-esteem through the early grades of elementary school. And my third was born with Down syndrome. Nothing she did in the school system was typical. She initiated the need for locks on the kindergarten room doors leading to the outside. She wore costumes to school. She danced and sang in the hallways. And in high school, she was the water girl for the senior boys' football team.

I second-guessed myself on choices we made for each of them, but I tried with each choice, each new challenge, to look at them like individuals. I advocated for them. But I didn't do everything for them. They had to learn their own way. Children are a product of their environment, but they are also born as tiny perfect individuals.

As I navigated parenthood by being present in the ups and downs, maybe these stories will help you on your journey.

Accept Your Imperfection

We are always the most careful with our firstborn. I remember hearing a comedian talk about how a soother (pacifier) for your first would be changed regularly, sterilized, and thrown out if it fell in the dirt, but by your third, if you dropped one, you would ask the dog to fetch it and bring it back. That's probably true to some degree. Although, with my first, I remember the devastation I felt when I arrived home with my then husband with groceries and things to put away. My daughter was in a car seat asleep, so we carefully placed it up on the kitchen island to keep her from being bothered by the dogs. Someone didn't quite put the car seat fully on the countertop, and she toppled to the floor. She was only a few months old. She was strapped in, and she wasn't hurt, but I sat and held her in my arms and cried for an hour. That was the first of many parenting blunders.

My son struggled in school with reading, but did have the advantage of great memorization skills that helped him out tremendously. That talent developed long before school. When he was only about three, he had the funniest little high-pitched voice and difficulty with pronouncing the R sound. The movie *Austin Powers* was out, and he had memorized a whole scene that he began to recite while standing on the seat of our booth in a restaurant. It was about a character named *Fat Bastard*. First mistake: He shouldn't have seen the movie. I thought he was too young to understand most of the humor in the movie, but I didn't anticipate his keen memory. Second mistake: I shouldn't have encouraged him with my laughter at home (and I probably shouldn't have laughed when he recited it in public). I've never been good at that kind of discipline when my kids were embarrassingly funny. They swore; I laughed.

Admit to Your Mistakes

I've apologized to my kids for everything from eating their Halloween treats, to leaving their father, to not leaving him soon enough. It's okay to be wrong. It's not okay to pretend you're always right.

The best thing you can do for your relationship with your child is admit your mistakes. I remember when the days of recordable DVDs came out. My then husband and my brother-in-law were both pretty tech savvy, and it wasn't long until we learned how to burn movies and play them in our DVD player (I know, in the world of multiple streaming sources, some of you reading this can't relate, but it was a thing!). It was my children who pointed out to me that recording movies in that fashion was stealing. I stopped and apologized to them and thanked them for setting me straight.

I recall, on a more serious note, when my oldest was going through some tough times in her teens. I thought we had a good relationship. I was in an unstable marriage, but continued to put on the united front when it came to parenting. It got to a point in my marriage where me and my children all felt unsafe at times. I was to discover later that caused her to feel unsafe with me, too. I was sure to apologize to her. Once I knew their safety was at risk, the decision to leave became so much easier. But I still had to apologize. I had to let her know that what I thought was the right parenting thing to do, was not. Our relationship now is built on trust, and I'm so thankful.

Be Flexible

I made a choice with my youngest child not to join the typical Down syndrome support communities available locally and in larger provincial and Canadian factions. I didn't want my child to think her life could only exist inside that community. I've realized I missed out on information and opportunities, but I also think she's well-adjusted and sees herself as part of the larger world around her.

She took gymnastics for many years. Her coach and I began to talk about her moving into Special Olympics competitions. That same spring, when lessons were coming to a close for the summer, she decided, since she had learned how to do a cartwheel and a somersault, she was finished! I was disappointed, because I thought she could go on to do more. But she was done. That's one of countless instances I could recite for any of my three children. They grow into and out of hobbies and interests as fast as clothes. We have to remember it's their dream. Little did I know, she would find herself many years later participating with great success in Special Olympic swimming as her focus and with great competence.

This child, now a young adult, has adopted herself into the family of the Jonas Brothers and lives out much of her day in imaginary interaction with them. She has a crazy imagination I would never want to quell. We have chats about trying to leave them at home when we go out in public and spending time with real people in her life when they are available. I feel like it's her coping mechanism for not having the family she would like to have. I've been separated from her father for over ten years, and that doesn't match the Disney picture of a family she sees on many movies and television shows. But there are upsides. This family influence somehow provides her with a conscience and maturity (I know, how can she act mature with an imaginary family?). She has taken on doing chores around the house without being asked. "They" have given her a set bedtime. She does work in schoolbooks each morning. These are all at the suggestion of her family. The things I've been trying to get her to do for years, she suddenly has stepped into at their behest. I'm flexible. If it's working somehow to move her forward in life, I'll take it!

Embrace Change

This is a little different than flexibility. This is the inevitable shift in character and circumstance that can be one of the hardest parts of parenting. The first indication in the early teen years when they don't want to be seen with you is the first dagger in your heart. Being a good parent is teaching your kids how to leave you.

My son attended a college program about four hours away from home. I'm not sure why I never knew that would be such a significant change. There should be some parenting guidelines through all phases of your child's life like they offer you for those first few years. You know: the timeline for first words, first steps, and potty training. Guideposts for older children could include being offered their first cigarette, when they ask for a cell phone, or when they go away to college, they don't come back.

Heartbreak. I wasn't ready for that. There were many appropriate and valid reasons why he wouldn't return home. It all made sense, but I had to work through the sadness and self-doubt to smile and help him move into his new space, new employment, and new life. I had to give him the space to grow. Give that space. But don't ever think they don't need you.

Keep Asking

Be sure they know they can tell you anything. It might be a stolen kiss at a tender young age or a financial crisis in their mid-forties. Keep asking if they're okay. Keep asking if they need you. Be sure it's genuine. I had a mother-in-law who always wanted to help, even if we didn't need it, so she could feel needed. It's about being available to them, not making yourself feel better.

We all want our children to be happy. When many of us don't know what our own happiness is, we can give advice through the wrong lens. We are taught to get a good education, find a good job, get married, have kids, retire, and die. That's not for everyone. That's probably not for most people, truthfully. I encouraged my one child to quit his job and start his own business in construction right at the start of everything closing down and people isolating in their homes at the onset of the Covid pandemic measures. Because he needed a sounding board. It was evident he needed to do it. So, I was there cheering him on.

I have times now, living with one adult child who returned home and one not yet ready to leave the nest, when I feel alone in the house with the three of us there. They have their own interests and schedules. I'm busy with work, renovating, and gardening. Often, our paths barely cross in a day.

There are times when my little one needs to snuggle in bed during a thunderstorm or hold my hand in the car. There are times when I change my schedule on the fly because the other one needs to talk about life. Most decisions are made without my input. Guidance is not sought and not kindly received when offered. But other times, there is the need for a soft place to land. I want to always be that. I still want to be in it, no matter how old I am and how old they are. That's my place. To show up the best I can in each moment and just be a parent. Embrace their personalities, honor my flaws, anticipate a vast array of problems, and just be ready to throw love at everything. Every action, when flavored with unconditional love, needs no explanation or apology. Just be in it.

Helen Snell

Helen Snell is a storyteller. She shows us that we each have a story and provides content that connects that story to your client's journey to create clear marketing strategies and develop relationships that close sales. As a copywriter and ghostwriter, she understands your credentials don't jump off a page, but your personality does. Helen uses her expertise to develop biographies and profiles, web content, marketing materials, blogs, and books. She also teaches the structure of clear communication and storytelling in workshops for those who want to master their writing craft. She is a certified communication coach and an international bestselling author and speaker. Many of her stories come from parenting her three children, being in nature, and being mastered by her dogs. Her audacious dreams include writing a book series for special needs adults and living on a sustainable property.

Connect with Helen at https://linktr.ee/helenharwoodsnell.

CHAPTER 6

Tips from a Punk Rock Doc

J.J. Kelly, Psy.D.

Well! Welcome to the show! I'm Dr. J.J. Kelly, The Punk Rock Doc, and I'm happy to meet ya! Everybody asks me what the punk means here, which … C'mon! What the punk do you think it means? Maybe it means I got the doctorate (with loans), did the training, worked in a prestigious group and private practice doin' psychotherapy and psychoeducation under a mainstream-ish model for seventeen years, and now, being the most-skilled clinician I know, I've found a more effective model for helpin' people get calm and happy. Maybe it means I did twelve years of Catholic school in the Midwest, and now I've got the foulest mouth in Northern California. Punk is counterculture, but not merely the opposite of everybody else. There's conformity, anti-conformity, and that sweet spot in between—*non*conformity.

Punk is whatever it wants to be. I am exactly who I want to be. And I teach people who want to learn to be exactly who they want to be. So, in a word, I teach freedom—which means I teach people how to experience a greater capacity for joy, regardless of what environment they're in or what big emotions they're feeling. Sounds good, Doc … but how?

First, let me just say, though I teach geniuses of all ages—corporate execs, ivy-league students and graduates, musical prodigies, formerly unhappy famous people, et cetera—the adolescents are my fave, and I consider that ages ten-ish to thirty-ish. Second, that pandemic! Holy *shit*, right? Well, from my shrink point of view, the pandemic illuminated the fact that *nobody* has any emotional intelligence skills, and we need 'em. So, people of all ages asked for help—which is productive. But they flooded what I consider to be a deeply flawed mental health system full of "isms"—not so productive.

So now all the psychotherapists—even the shitty ones—are totally full-up, for a while, probably since that's the traditional model. And people wanting skills and change in their lives are paying through the nose for weekly whatever, and if it's subpar, the client is most likely wondering what *they're* doin' wrong. Lemme tell ya: nothin'. If you're not being taught the skills and makin' *marked* changes in your daily/weekly behaviors, and you're not being challenged about that … LEAVE. Don't keep payin' for nada. And if you're a member of a non-majority community, *of any kind* … this—times a million.

I've taught Dialectical Behavior Therapy (DBT) since 2004, and now I teach it exclusively: eight weeks, four modules of emotional intelligence skills, and tons of change. If you don't know what a dialectic is, don't sweat it. It's just a fancy term for a kind of paradox or contradiction—two seemingly opposites things existing in an integrated and harmonious way. Like how the balanced overlap of conformity and anti-conformity births *non*conformity. That two-circle Venn diagram represents how Zen Mindfulness blends with Cognitive Behavior Therapy (CBT) to create the overlap of DBT. The mindfulness piece is what No-Problem Parenting wants me to address with you.

Mindfulness is definitely gaining some mainstream momentum—celebrities talking about their TM (Transcendental Meditation), Jon Kabat-Zinn stress-management stuff, and T-shirts that say, "Keep Calm…" Puke. What's wonderful and useful about mindfulness training is how it slows down the fast-paced reactionary shit that turns small mistakes into big messes. Think about it: yer cruisin' along, mindin' yer own business, and something unexpected and shitty happens that "triggers" you. Ugh ... I'm so over people using that word—like, weaponizing it. "What you said was a trigger for me …" Like, *I'm* supposed to guess what your triggers are and adjust my behaviors accordingly? Most of us have trauma, and our triggers are *our* responsibility, folx! And that may mean verbalizing "Please don't do [that thing you just did that triggered me]. It makes me angry." And inform the person, giving them a chance to adjust their behavior, if they're willing.

The core mindfulness skills (module one of four in DBT) is the backbone of the model—as is the concept of validation. We validate all the emotions we experience—not all thoughts, but yes, all emotional experiences. Validation, in a nutshell, just means acknowledging the emotion we're having right now—we notice it and we name it. Simple, right? You'd think so, but many very smart people I have worked with have a shockingly primitive vocabulary for their emotions. Nope, high IQ does not automatically translate to high EQ (emotional intelligence). In fact, smart people have really smart rationalizations for avoiding their true emotions. It's still bullshit, but it's smart bullshit. What I tell people is, bullshit is a skill set. Everybody does it sometimes—to minimize consequences, to get their needs met, et cetera. But I want you to *know* you're using it and use it sparingly, so you don't erode your integrity and self-esteem. Remember, it's all about making sure your actions match your values. And mindfulness helps you to slow down and notice when you are … and when you're not.

I want to teach you a couple of mindfulness exercises your family can put into practice *right now* that will both increase your EQ and positively impact your interactions with your kids, teens, and young adults. First, go to drjjkelly.com and on that home page, all the way to the right, is a paper clip icon. Click on that, and you'll be offered two versions of our Feelings Sheet. Print that out and put it on the fridge. Now, if any conflict arises—intense or mild—ask your kiddo what they're feeling and have them pick some emotion words from the sheet. You can do it, too, to model moving through the emotion and validating it by naming it. Again, this sounds simple … but it takes practice for it to become automatic and easy to do. Using the sheet to name emotions serves several purposes at once:

- A practice of naming emotions increases our emotions vocabulary, which facilitates
- Taking responsibility for our own emotional experience (which reduces blame) and
- Slowing down reactivity and distracting from the intensity of the emotion by engaging the brain in the productive exercise of going to the sheet to find your emotions, and finally
- Getting the whole family on the same page of how we engage with our emotions and the emotions of others—we now have a common language and practice that unites us as a family.

You will be surprised at the intensity and positivity of the impact of this simple family exercise. The kid'll fight you on it at first, but if you stick to it and model it for them by doing it yourself when you're with them, it'll become old hat in no time.

There are some key tips to remember when using the Feelings Sheet. I had you print out the one from my website because the feelings lists or wheels online contain a ton of thoughts masquerading as feelings, and that is counterproductive. Shrinks are for sure to blame for this trend of botched "I feel …" statements.

For instance: "I feel like you're an asshole." *Not* a statement of feelings. "… like you're an asshole" is not a feeling—it's a thought. It's an opinion. It's a judgment… not to mention, name-calling, which is not allowed when working with me. I got this example from doin' couples therapy years ago, and it's a perfect example of what *not* to do. A judgment is anything with an evaluative quality: right/wrong, good/bad, worthwhile/worthless. These are definitely thoughts, not feelings, and in working with me, we minimize or eliminate statements like this. You are still entitled to an opinion; just state it as an opinion, then.

So many people try to pass off judgments and opinions as facts. They're not facts, they're just your opinions. And an opinion statement starts with, "I think …" So, in the example, "I feel like you're an asshole"—that's an opinion. The way to know is if the words immediately following the word "feel" is "like" or "that." If it's a true statement of feeling, the word immediately following the work "feel" would be an emotion word: happy, sad, angry, embarrassed, et cetera. Get it? So, I might have an opinion (without name-calling) and say, "I think you're acting like an asshole." Or, better yet, own it by saying "I don't like how you're acting. Please stop." But if you're going to make it a true feeling statement, it'd be more like "I feel really pissed when you do that. Please stop." This is oversimplified, but I cannot stress how often this mistake happens in real life.

Oh, and by the way, "attacked" is not a feeling. It's a judgement and, therefore, automatically a thought. When someone says "I feel attacked" in response to me challenging their beliefs (which is my job), they are guessing at what my intention is. You cannot state that I'm attacking you unless I, first, confirm that I am. I get around it by saying "If you *think* I'm attacking you, how would you feel?" The feeling is what we're after here—and when you validate it by saying "pissed" or "scared" or whatever, I have no argument. I do, however, take issue with your inference that my intention is to attack you.

And most people, once they're calm, definitely know I am helping them through change and not attacking them—it's just that fear often tricks us into blaming or demonizing others, which is a shame. So much of conflict is misunderstanding in the moment of activated emotions. That's why this exercise is so important to all families—and all people. When we increase our emotional intelligence, we get more and more specific in how we use language and communicate. This reduces misunderstanding and increases effective communication and connection. So, we eliminate thoughts from our feelings vocabulary; interested, unsure, unsafe, attacked, good, bad are not feelings. We replace them with actual emotions like excitement, uneasiness, fear, happiness, panic, et cetera, so we can understand each other and develop a deeper understanding of ourselves, what we feel and why, and *where* in our body we feel our feelings.

We have *so much* room to grow in the area of emotional intelligence, and I am happy to be a teacher out there helping those who want to learn because it is my belief that global healing is achieved by teaching people the skills to like themselves. Or, as I like to put it:

Happy People Act Right!

Hope you've enjoyed learning these few tips, and if you have questions, you know where to find me!

Dr. J.J. Kelly

Dr. J.J. Kelly is a licensed clinical psychologist and emotional intelligence skills training expert. J.J. is also the CEO and founder of UnorthoDocs, Inc., a punk alternative to traditional psychotherapy. Dr. Kelly and the unortho"docs" live their lives with the belief that global healing is achieved by teaching people the skills to like themselves.

Connect with J.J. Kelly at www.drjjkelly.com.

CHAPTER 7

Creating Vulnerable Conversations Through Divorce

Joy Bartholomew

Nothing can prepare you for the moment your spouse says that he loves someone else and that he won't stop seeing her. Your mind spins. Your heart aches. Your breath stops. And your world is turned completely upside down.

That was my response when my husband came to me after a day out on our family boat with one of my close girlfriends and all of our kids.

I knew in my heart that something wasn't right, so I declined to go with them earlier in the day. When I asked him later that night about her, he didn't lie or sugar-coat it. He answered plainly and clearly, like he'd been rehearsing the lines for weeks, even months. And even though I knew the answer, hearing the words float in the warm night air still cut like a knife directly into my heart.

As you begin to move forward from that moment in time, when your life changes forever, you work through the grief – the denial, the hurt, and the anger. Then you finally resign yourself to the truth that it's over; it's time to heal and move on.

Except divorce isn't just an emotional transition and healing journey that you walk through alone, it's a time of transition for everyone in the family. It's learning how to manage your own emotions and help your kids with their emotions as well. It's not a time to be singularly focused on your own pain, but a time to heal as a family.

When divorce hits, it takes a toll on the whole family. No one is immune to the effects. Often it creates tension, conflict, emotional outbursts and erratic behavior, adults and kids alike; and everyone processes it differently. It takes work by every member of the family to foster the parent-child relationship during separation and divorce. And with patience, understanding and effective communication, these bonds between parent and child can be maintained and grow even deeper.

My daughter was 12 and my son was 14 when the separation occurred in our family. Too young to know all the sordid details, but far too old to be given poor excuses. It was finding balanced and authentic conversations to help them through the process. It was giving them the stability, support and love they needed, with small doses of genuine truths, so they could start their grief and healing journey.

It wasn't just me that was hurting, it was them as well. I had to learn to put myself aside at times and truly become the parent, the stoic, the rock that they needed. Sometimes they truly needed to rely on my strength.

Being unflappable was a façade. Being strong only lasted so long. And holding back the dam of tears and overwhelming emotions finally had to break. It was in those moments where we could open up and talk together, be raw and vulnerable, be humble and honest, that we connected on that deeper and more personal level.

Allowing them to see my hurt over the separation helped them become more open with their pain as well. Seeing me struggle with my emotions allowed them to feel more relief that they weren't alone in their own emotional unease.

It was when my daughter was 16, that she had a moment of insight and came to me with questions. "So, when we went on that last family vacation, the summer right before the separation, and I brought my friend … you already knew that dad was having an affair with her mom?"

"Yes. Yes, I did know. But it wasn't your fault, or your friend's fault, and I couldn't hold that against either of you. So yes, I knew about the affair and still allowed her to come with us."

This conversation came after years of opportunities to connect and talk openly. This was a bond forged over movie-night whispered conversations and car ride sing-alongs and talks. It wasn't a conversation for a 12-year-old girl in the midst of turmoil, but it was more suited for a 16-year-old young woman, who is eager to begin a life of her own. A life of relationships that she would have to learn to traverse. The pain of a break-up. The sting of betrayal. The frustration after an argument. The in-depth conversations that could bring about reconciliation. Or the ability to walk away from someone who wasn't suited for her. Whether these were romantic relationships or deep-rooted friendships, she needed to understand how to handle and cope with the ups and downs; how to have unguarded conversations and communicate effectively.

I hadn't been a great communicator growing up or in my marriage. I hadn't spoken up for myself, and I was finding post-marriage that it created more problems by keeping quiet. It created more personal difficulties by going-along for the sake of getting-along. It was during this time that I found my voice, spoke my truth, and grew more confident. It hadn't been a skill set that I had mastered and if you haven't mastered it either, that's okay. This is a great time to start making changes for the benefit of yourself and your kids.

Small changes lead to the biggest results. It's why I became a divorce and life coach, and why I work with women during this pivotal time of divorce. I learned there was true power in the building blocks of incremental small changes to make big transformations in our lives. It's not the quick-footed hare that wins the race overnight, it's the tortoise-slow habits we live day-in and day-out that create the life and connections we truly crave. And if you're craving a stronger relationship with your kids, you can make that happen, but it's starting, like I did, with those first steps to bring about honest conversations and true connections that bring those steadfast relationships to fruition.

I found that if I wanted to bond with my kids on a deeper level and build the best relationship possible, then I had to create trust and encourage openness. It had to start with me. I had to learn how to model that healthy and open communication style that I had run from for so long. I had to really talk to my kids; not the typical surface level of *everything is fine* platitudes. I had to model *real talk* with real emotions. Having these conversations isn't easy and it may not feel natural, but your kids will appreciate the honesty.

These conversations were anchored in truth and love. These weren't conversations based on angry emotions that may unknowingly hurt or alienate them or separate them from their dad. These were personal feelings of pain, frustration, or sadness. We, as a family, had dreams, and with the landscape of our family changing it's no wonder how these emotions come into the equation. Even if your kids aren't saying them, they're feeling them, too. They're feeling uncertainty, hurt and anger. Their lives have been upended as well.

"Things are changing. Our family is changing. We aren't going to live together anymore, and our everyday lives are changing. I'm sad over those changes, and sometimes angry. And it's okay to be sad. It's okay be mad. It wasn't what I had anticipated or wanted for us as a family. But we, as mom and dad, still love you and that will never change!"

This wasn't to use my kids as pseudo-therapists or to dump drama onto them. This wasn't about being a victim. This was an opportunity to speak to my kids at an age-appropriate level to allow them to feel comfortable with their own feelings and allow them to voice their concerns and hurts.

It took time for them to process their feelings and put them into words, and I had to be willing to allow them space to sort them out. I couldn't nag with questions and force conversations out of them, though there were times I felt I needed to know what was going on in that moment. Often, they couldn't put those feelings into words yet or weren't ready to verbalize their hurts, anxieties, or fears. It can feel that they are closed off, and being aware of their mental and emotional state is important, but allowing them quiet solitude to process what is happening, the impact to their lives and their personal feelings can give them a better grasp on how to communicate it.

When they were ready, we were able to open a dialogue where they could feel comfortable asking questions and learning more. And sometimes those questions were hard to answer, either due to the adult facts or to the personal emotions involved, but I had to lay the foundation of truth and answer as honestly and fully as possible to build trust. Half answers or partial truths can be felt as inauthentic, and close communication down. Even making statements, such as, "yes, there is more, but it's not my place to share that part of the story, it's not fully mine to tell" or "Here's what I can tell you now, but we need to talk about that other part at a later time, there is so much involved that I'm still working through myself and isn't yet completely known." Telling them what you can and limiting, with reason, what you can't, can give your child a feeling of information fulfillment and protection.

As those conversations continued, it was my turn to listen – actively listen. To be fully present with no distractions. No phone calls, no text messages, no television. To be engaged in the moment, those fleeting moments of true connection with my children. Sometimes they ended in laughs, sometimes in tears. But it built that connection, conversation-by-conversation, that I was available to them, no matter the circumstances.

I learned to listen to their point of view. Though it may have been different from my own, it was still valid. Though it may have been difficult to hear at times, I had to hear their truth. It's their perspective and it's their experience, and I couldn't take from that. I had to be open to their experiences. It gave an opportunity for them to truly communicate what they were thinking and feeling. It gave us better insight into one another, to grow together.

I had to listen without judgement. It may be hard for them to say something that could be painful and be harder for me to hear, but I am the parent – I am the adult. I had to learn to listen and allow them to express themselves honestly. Ground rules needed to be set for respectful conversations, but if they were mad at me, I had to be a big girl and listen to the basis of their anger. Because if I can't be open to hearing it, they'll feel there isn't any safe space or any opportunity to share. They'll mislead or lie or under-report their emotions if they believe they'll only be criticized or feel their emotions aren't being viewed as valid.

Those bits of misinformation in conversations create cracks in the foundation. Those times the answer is "I'm fine," when it clearly isn't, widens the fissures just a little bit more. Those critical responses, rather than ones of understanding, deepen the ravines. These make it harder to mend relationships, and it doesn't serve to build a better connection.

No matter the circumstance. No matter the misunderstanding. No matter what. I've always wanted my kids to know I've got their back. That they can come to me with anything. That I will listen. That I love them. And that together we can solve any problem.

Sometimes I think about it in my head and know it in my heart, but I don't often say the words out loud enough. They need to hear the words and see the example of this lived out daily to rely on it as solid truth.

One of the sayings we had in my house growing up was my parents would ask, "What do you always remember, and never forget?" To which my response was always, "Mommy and Daddy love me."

I've continued that saying with my own kids. And though it's been a while since they last recited it, I know it's engrained in their being, that mommy and daddy love them. So, no matter where I fall short in my communication or managing my emotions, I always want them to know that love is the basis to rely on.

Creating a new life after divorce can be complicated with managing so many emotions, keeping up with obligations, establishing new routines, and learning to co-parent. Building a better relationship with your kids during this phase takes patience, time, and communication. You can't force it, but you can encourage and build it, step-by-step. You offer opportunities for quiet time and personal space so they can process emotions and feelings. You offer quality time where together you can foster that connection and closeness. All in a space of respect and love. Through these vulnerable conversations we can continue to grow that relationship and deepen that connection.

Joy Bartholomew

Joy Bartholomew is a divorced mom with 2 independent college kids and 2 loveable fur babies.

During her divorce, Joy struggled to find her way as a single woman and mom. Through the roller coaster of emotions, Joy knew there had to be a better way to make the transition back into single life with less stress.

After a 30-year career in law enforcement, Joy became certified as a 500-hour yoga teacher, a meditation facilitator, and a divorce-life-resilience coach. She then opened The Divorce Confidante, as a divorce coach and podcaster. Her goal now is to be a resource for midlife women and moms who need support through their divorce and co-parenting journey and on to an abundant life full of possibilities and freedom.

Joy is stepping into her next adventure as a coach, writer, podcaster, and speaker. She can be found at www.divorce-confidante.com.

Joy lives outside of Charleston, SC. She shares a home with her golf-loving mom, Sherry.

"When you go through deep waters, I will be with you. When you go through rivers of difficulty, you will not drown. When you walk through the fire of oppression, you will not be burned up; the flames will not consume you. For I am the Lord, your God, the Holy One of Israel, your Savior." Isaiah 43:2-3a NLT.

Connect with Joy at www.divorce-confidante.com.

CHAPTER 8

Five Be-Attitudes of Hope for Parents

Julie Kenzler

Having no knowledge about how to raise a child at the age of twenty-seven, I did what most new moms do and bought the book, *What to Expect the First Year* by Heidi Murkoff. It's a mighty good thing she wrote the next one, *What to Expect the Second Year*, because I still didn't feel like a pro. Somehow, in the third year, I became a master at momming and didn't need any more *What to Expect* type books. Well, the truth is that I became too busy to read those big books and did a lot of trial and, err, and prayer.

My four amazing children are grown up, and at times, I contemplate how I could have done this or done that, or not done this or not done that. Or I could have done *more* of that or *less* of this. You get the picture. *Regrets!* This is a big challenge we parents face as our children move into their own paths and directions that take them away from home. By the way, nobody told me how hard it would be to raise children, the physical and emotional output every day. That same *nobody* also forgot to tell me how challenging it would be emotionally to let go when they grow up. On the one hand, I wish I knew what I know now; I would have treasured the messy and chaotic moments so much more. But I also may have had fewer children, knowing the deep grief we go through when they leave the nest.

Parenting is such a beautiful work. It is unique to our own experiences, dreams, and desires. Like a snowflake, no two parents *parent* the same way. Without a doubt, though, parenting is hard work that blesses our socks off. It's the ultimate roller-coaster ride as you click that seatbelt and hold onto the bar, screaming and hands flying around. Dr. James Dobson says it best with his book titled, *Parenting Isn't for Cowards*.

Allow me to introduce the *BE-attitudes of Parenting* to scatter a little hope on you:

- Be life-giving
- Be still
- Be courageous
- Be steadfast
- Be vulnerable

Be Life-Giving - Resist Being a Critical Parent

As parents, we find ourselves using words of correction, criticism, and redirection to train and guide our children from the early ages to the uncertain teenage years. Our sincere intentions are pure in guiding these little humans, but I realized much later that my words caused hurt. Negative, critical words can cause self-doubt and insecurity. They undermine confidence and alter self-image. Even worse, negative words can damage relationships.

I created a positive, fun, and loving home for my children, but I did use more critical and correcting words than I like to recall. When faced with challenging moments and seasons in parenting, though, staying positive and speaking life-giving words is not easy. Still, what children want and need most is a cheerleader parent.

Learning more about positive words and the connection they have to a grateful heart has helped me make a vital shift to speaking life-giving words to my children. Retraining my brain from negative to positive takes effort, like training for a sport. And this is not just any sport; it's parenting.

Instead of saying "You're not going to wear that outfit, are you? It's wrinkled and isn't the best color on you," try "You have a great smile, and I know you will be such a light at the event tonight. People love to hang out with you." Who really cares about the outfit anyway? We tend to get hung up on such minor things; on the contrary, let's focus on the major things, like our child's confidence and character.

Remember, man does not live on bread alone: sometimes he needs a little buttering up. ~ John Maxwell, pastor and author

---

Be Still - Pause and Observe

I can't even count how many times I jumped to conclusions with my children and spoke or reacted before understanding the situation completely. A child comes home after curfew, and our natural reaction is to assume the worst. Why didn't I first ask them to explain the reason? How does it help to reactively say, "You lost the car for one week." Instead, I propose we take a step back and observe what is happening. Let's see from their perspective. Is there a deeper issue or hurt they might be dealing with?

When faced with challenges as a parent, we often respond and react instead of pause. Pause. Be still. Google told me *pause* means *a temporary stop in action or speech.* The sentence example given was this: *She dropped me outside during a brief pause in the rain.* I am laughing hysterically at this visual! Where was the person dropped from? I'm glad they waited until the pause in the rain. But if it was a hot day, the rain may have been quite refreshing anyway. You see, I don't know the full context of that sentence and can assume many things. I need the full story before I can decide my opinion of someone getting dropped in the non-rain.

Sending the message that we want to *hear* our child is powerful. Taking time, being still, and leaning into a more observant role will add trust and strength to the parent-child relationship.

Your home needs to be a place where your kids can fail—and learn from their failure. Surround them with love, show them how important they are to you, but don't try to undo their failures. It's not our job as parents to get our kids off the hook. ~ Kevin Leman, psychologist and author

---

Be Courageous - Trust Your Instincts and Your Heart

Teaching four teenagers to drive a vehicle (with gas in it) on the road with hundreds of other cars is no easy task. There are consistently moments in parenting when we need to make hard decisions, but second-guess ourselves. In those moments, allowing courage and trust to guide our steps may not be easy, but they are solid navigational tools for parenting: courage to stand firm or give in a little more than our comfort zone allows and trust to believe our decision is what is best for our child despite their pushback or disapproval.

My son, Jack, was about three years old, and my husband planned a surprise trip to the beach in California for our anniversary. He arranged for friends to take our son for the weekend and for an elaborate dinner reservation for us, overlooking the ocean at sunset. Wow, what a dream trip with a dream husband. Not for this young momma who had not left her child except for quick errands. I was terrified! My husband had my bag packed and began to drive toward our destination. I thought it was to a resort in the Phoenix area and began to panic as we drove to the airport. It took only courage and trust in my husband, our friends, and God's peace to help me go on this trip. Though we did return a day early, I have that memory in my heart as a wonderful celebration with my husband and proof I can do hard things as a parent.

If parenting were an adventure sport, it would be the most courageous sport in the world. It involves venturing into the unknown, full of unexpected twists and turns, and is completely unpredictable. It is also thrilling and rewarding. Parenting is by far my boldest adventure. ~ Mandi Hart, author

---

Be Steadfast - Don't Give Up

How many times in life is something so hard for us, and when we overcome it, we have grown and look back and say, "Wow, that wasn't so bad after all." Starting a new job, moving to a new town, working on home repair, and healing from surgery to name a few. Just when it seems too hard to continue, that is when we can make a switch from hopelessness and exhaustion to grit and hope. Remain steadfast and never give up.

As a mom, I can't begin to count the number of times I felt like throwing in the towel and going on a thirty-day sabbatical. It seemed most often when my children weren't listening to me, running late in the mornings, or showing disrespect. A wise teacher for my teenage son Ryan explained it so well. "He's in the tunnel, but will get through it. Stay consistent with what you are doing as a parent."

Ryan grew despondent to me in his teen years. When I was a substitute teacher at my children's school, he avoided me at all costs. Not even a hello. As he gained more independence, he had a careless attitude, causing me many worried nights.

My weekly prayer meeting was consistent over the years, praying for all my children, but especially for Ryan and his rebelliousness. I was missing the son I had. On a particularly difficult night, Ryan ran out of the house with his Bible and guitar. Immediately, my husband and I knelt to pray by our bed, crying out to God for our son to return home, physically and emotionally.

Fifteen minutes later, we heard the door fly open; Ryan ran upstairs sobbing. He read a Bible verse that opened his eyes to how he had been treating us. We embraced and cried tears of relief and hope. Today, Ryan is a successful marketing expert and is strong and confident. He has a wonderful community with his church. Most of all, he has a growing relationship with God and a very close relationship with his dad and me. A redemption story that healed the wounds in my heart.

Stay steadfast. You never know when the turning point is around the corner.

The attitude you have as a parent is what your kids will learn. They don't remember what you try to teach them. They remember who you are. ~ Jim Henson, creator of The Muppets

---

Be Vulnerable - Don't Face Challenges Alone

I quickly learned that parents don't need to live in a glass castle, but they can't thrive living in a cave either. We need one another. One person's struggle to victory is another person's hope in challenging times. It is in a community where we are encouraged, inspired, and cheered on. Find that close friend who can be your confidante. Talk about the struggles openly at your comfort level. Let them pray for you and be the shoulder to cry on. Find a support group or counselor who can guide you in the more difficult times. Don't go it alone.

In my Hope Follows broadcasts, I interview people about their life struggles and the hope that followed. One gentleman named Alex made life choices as a teenager that put his family through major testing. His mother and father talked about the hardships, worries, and need for support. They had to be open with their prayer group, family, and professional support programs in order to journey through that treacherous path of watching their son sabotage his life.

Hope Follows! Oh, the story is so sweet today. Alex is thriving and has grown close to his parents once again. They have received healing. But it didn't happen with his parents staying isolated and alone. They had to be vulnerable. When you need someone to talk with, reach out to that trusted family member or friend.

Vulnerability is not winning or losing; it's having the courage to show up and be seen when we have no control over the outcome. Vulnerability is not weakness; it's our greatest measure of courage. ~ Brene Brown, professor and author

---

Whatever stage of parenting you are in, try these five be-attitudes of parenting as merely one more tool in your toolbox for becoming the best hope-filled version of you.

Serenity Prayer
God grant me the serenity to accept the things
I cannot change, courage to change the things I can,
and the wisdom to know the difference.

Julie Kenzler

Julie Kenzler is an avid writer and promoter of finding "HOPE" in all the hard things we face in life. Her blog writing journey led to her first published book, *Hope Follows*, in 2020. Julie is a contributing author in the bestselling book *Lemonade Stand Book #3: The Path from Sour to Sweet*, published in 2023.

Behind a camera and mic as an international broadcaster and podcaster, Julie brings people's hope-filled stories to 7 continents and 190 countries through the Holy Spirit Broadcasting Network and Christian Women's Word Network on Amazon Fire TV, LG, Facebook, Roku, YouTube, and Spotify. You will laugh and cry only to find inspiration and courage with Julie and her guests, determined to find your HOPE FOLLOWS story in the midst of challenges you face.

Whether it is a room filled with a captive audience or on a stage, Julie's voice of experience and charm brings authority to teaching those around her to have confidence and boldness in reclaiming lost joy.

God has been her anchor and rock in walking through some difficult and dark days to living a joyful life. Her heart fills up to the brim anytime she spends time with her husband and adult children by a campfire, on a hiking trail, or playing board games. Making memories is her proclamation with the motto "Carpe Omnia!" Seize it all!

Connect with Julie at www.hopefollows.com.

CHAPTER 9

Cultivating Your Child's Strengths Within Her Own Unique Context

Kate K. Lund, Psy.D.

Imagine a little girl with big glasses and a funny-looking haircut sitting on the outside of the group because the other kids are laughing at how she looks. Sadly, this is a common experience for kids who look and feel different from others. I know this because I was that little girl. The reality of my early experience and that of so many other kids has been reinforced time and again in my work as a clinical psychologist.

At an age when kids just want to fit in, and not stand out, I often faced the world with a partially shaved head (this was before side-and under-shaves became trendy), big glasses, and a heavy hockey helmet when skating with my class. All of this was because I was living with Hydrocephalus, a medical condition in which cerebral spinal fluid doesn't circulate as it should, causing pressure to build up on the brain. All this meant lots of time in the hospital and surgery to fix my shunt (which circulates my cerebral spinal fluid for me), lots of missed school and lots of time looking and feeling different.

Thanks to parents and teachers who encouraged me to focus on what I could do as opposed to what I could not do or the things that made me different, I was able to find my own normal. Because of this, I learned to find joy in my own unique context and sense of possibilities.

It is incredibly empowering to teach kids to find what's ordinary and what's possible for them within the context of their own unique challenges and range of abilities. When kids accept and embrace their own unique context – what is normal for them, especially when they're going through challenges that are not typical for their age group or society, it becomes possible for them to develop their strengths, compensate for challenge, and focus on possibility. Living their ordinary is key to moving toward their full potential and ultimately finding their extraordinary.

From about the age of five to the age of twelve, children are at a critical developmental stage where their primary focus is on competence. They become aware of what kids their age are expected to be able to do, and they take great pride in their accomplishments when they live up to these expectations. Children who receive positive feedback for taking initiative and trying new things, even when they fail, grow into confident and resilient adults. Those who receive negative or very little feedback when they fail and are not encouraged to try again (or try something new) tend to develop feelings of inferiority.

A foundational lesson for kids to learn at this stage is that what's normal for them is different from what's normal for their siblings and their friends, and that this is ok. It can be difficult for kids to acknowledge limitations and challenges, but if they remain focused on what they can do as opposed to what they can't do, they will discover their own unique capabilities. This leads to a sense of possibility and opportunity. It is important to mention here that acknowledging and working through the challenges that exist is vital as we can't ignore the real challenges that our kids face.

This idea was exemplified beautifully by an adolescent girl I met when training in clinical psychology at a pediatric burn hospital. I was working with kids who had suffered catastrophic injuries. Their lives had been changed forever in ways that would be difficult to imagine. This young girl had lost her eyesight in a fire. She was surrounded by kids playing video games and board games, watching cartoons, and making silly faces at each other. Instead of focusing on the things she could no longer do, she continued to share an amazing gift that the fire had not been able to take from her—her voice. Everyone on that unit, patients, and staff alike, was blown away by her strong and heartfelt singing. She brought us together and reminded us of how much we all shared and how much we had to be grateful for.

I'm not saying that learning to be content with your own limitations is an easy lesson to learn, especially for a child. I know something about this from personal experience.

When I was eight years old, all I wanted was to be able to tumble around with the other kids, hang upside-down on the horizontal ladder, and compete in sports like hockey and softball. But this was not possible because of my hydrocephalus. I remember a birthday party where all the other kids were bouncing on a trampoline. I knew better, but I climbed onto that trampoline and bounced too. I felt so normal and free for a brief-moment, but then the world started spinning. I rolled off the trampoline and threw up, and I didn't stop throwing up for a week.

Throughout my childhood, despite my limitations, I enjoyed most of the activities that I wanted to try. Whenever I was able to participate in whatever game the other kids were playing, I was ecstatic. I longed to play contact sports, but those were off-limits.

It was my parents who gently helped me shift my attention away from the intangible and encouraged me to find something I could play safely and be passionate about. When they noticed how much I enjoyed throwing the ball for my dog to fetch, my dad started taking me to the tennis courts near our house. This became a ritual that we enjoyed together throughout my childhood. My Dad never made me feel like he had any grand expectations for me on the court. I was free to set my own goals and standards as I developed my skills. I practiced every chance I got and became a pretty good player.

I think part of the reason I enjoyed tennis so much was because it felt like I was doing my own thing. Even though I rarely won tournaments, I brought home numerous runner-up trophies, and that was fine. I knew that it was the best I could do within my own unique context. I played competitively enough and even made it to a few regional tournaments as the captain of my high school's team, but my deepest joy and satisfaction came from competing with myself, challenging myself to make each best match better than the last.

My parents instilled in me that one of the greatest values in playing the sports that I loved was in the lifelong friendships that I was building. I wasn't playing to win; I was playing for the joy of it. I was there to develop my skills, connect with my peers, and simply make the most of those priceless moments.

There were plenty of times when hydrocephalus kept me from playing. I got very sick with headaches and nausea, and there were lengthy hospital stays every time my shunt needed to be replaced or repositioned. I came to accept that as part of what was normal for me. Every time I could get out onto the court and face an opponent, I was so happy.

For any child, the ability to find their own ordinary and define their own normal opens possibility because it frees them up to ignore all of the external expectations for what's "normal" that don't apply to them. As parents and guardians, if we're always pushing our kids to do more and be more than who they really are, we're missing beautiful opportunities to allow them to be ordinary—whatever that looks like for them.

Here are some foundational ways we can help our kids come to terms with their limitations and make themselves at home within their own capabilities:

- Identify your child's strengths and maximize all opportunities for them to shine.
- Encourage your child to use their imagination to develop a vision for goals that they can realistically accomplish.
- Celebrate your child's wins, whether they're large or small. When they start to compare themselves negatively to their peers or to the expectations of others, refocus their attention on things they've done well and things that have gone right.
- Acknowledge their potential, praise their efforts, and point out areas where they have been improving.
- Encourage kids to move outside of their comfort zone and stretch the boundaries of what they believe they can do.
- Be clear, genuine, and realistic when you're giving a child praise and encouragement. Don't tell them they're good at something that doesn't match their abilities. Instead, let them know that you see and appreciate their efforts and their individual strengths for what they are.
- Model positive self-talk. Acknowledge your own strengths and accomplishments and those of other people in the child's life.
- Encourage children to develop and follow their own interests. By doing so, they are learning intrinsic motivation, a crucial

ingredient as they learn to recognize and maximize their potential.

- If you have a child who seems to excel at everything they do, encourage them to seek out new skills that will be more challenging so that when they get older, they will know how to face challenges.
- Another valuable gift you can give your child is to help them become resilient so that they can bounce back and either try again or try something new when things go wrong. Provide strategies for managing stress and tolerating frustrations so that when challenges arise, kids don't lose sight of what's going well and what they're doing right.
- Allow kids to struggle and persevere when they're facing challenges in an area that they're passionate about instead of trying to redirect them to a different activity. It can be difficult to watch your child repeatedly fall short, but keep in mind (and remind your child) that failure isn't the opposite of success, it's part of it. If they eventually decide to shift gears and try something different, honor the fact that they are acknowledging their own context for what's normal for them.
- It's important to help kids understand that making mistakes is a normal part of learning and to provide them with tools to help them learn from their mistakes. We can do this by:
    1. Encouraging them to keep trying, no matter how many times they fail, when they are working toward a realistic goal.
    2. Framing challenges as opportunities for growth and skill development.

3. Demonstrating that it's ok to make mistakes, try again after failure, and change course when faced with an impossible challenge.
4. Pointing out as role models people who persevered in order to gain competence and build confidence.
5. We can also demonstrate this important lesson by cultivating authentic and transparent relationships with our children. One way for them to learn that each person has their own normal and that it's ok not to succeed at everything you try right out of the gate is to share our own experiences of learning, struggling, failing, and persevering. I do this with my own fifteen-year-old boys who are figuring out where they fit in the world and where their truc strengths lie.

Showing kids that you believe in their abilities will go a long way in helping them develop confidence in their abilities. Through positive reinforcement and support, you can help kids develop the tools they need to succeed both now and, in the future, in whatever context they find themselves.

For me, as a child with hydrocephalus, what everyone else saw as ordinary seemed extraordinary. I rarely got to experience what most people considered normal. Finding my own normal, however, led to some incredible experiences that felt truly extraordinary. I learned to appreciate physical abilities that I might otherwise have taken for granted.

When a child learns to embrace their own unique context, they discover the gifts that they already have. They learn that no matter what challenges they face, their own intrinsic strength and resilience can help them to overcome and grow from those experiences.

Dr. Kate Lund

Dr. Kate Lund is a licensed clinical psychologist, peak performance coach, best-selling author and Tedx Speaker. She helps parents and children build resilience so they can thrive in school, sports, and life. During Kate's childhood, she faced and eventually overcame a difficult childhood illness, so she learned at an early age to believe in the possibility that exists on the other side of challenges.

Connect with Dr. Kate at www.katelundspeaks.com.

CHAPTER 10

Creating a Safe Container for Growth

Kay Chorna

I didn't plan on having children. It was never a dream of mine or a goal to get married and become a mom. I wanted a life of adventure, wild dreams, and freedom. Maybe it has to do with my rebellious spirit or maybe with the fact that my own childhood was far from ideal.

Life sometimes changes our trajectory.

In my twenties, I started peeling the onion of how my past impacted me, but by the time my thirties hit, I was deep into personal development and conscious living. I met my soulmate, we got married, and the desire to have a child with him was born within me.

I knew about the power of intention, so the first time we made love, without any protection, I got pregnant. It was easy, beautiful, and effortless.

During the whole pregnancy, I was focusing and learning about the birth itself—the birth of a child! To me, it was the most profound, deep, and intensely magical initiation of my life, from maiden to mother. It came with a lot of emotional and physical changes, and I learned everything I could possibly learn to achieve a natural, empowering birth. And I did! I truly believe in the power of manifestation and the incredible abilities our brain and heart have. The ability to create and cause the results we want in our lives, and in some cases, true miracles.

What I didn't think about, or learn about, is anything that happens *after* the birth. How to raise an actual human being. About all the intricacies of child-rearing, all the complexities of our relationship, and all the triggers that are going to come up for me while raising him.

I thought I was done healing! It's so comical looking back now, as my biggest healing happened *after* his birth, not before. In the ways that having a newborn child and then a toddler challenges you, it brings up everything that you might have overlooked, suppressed, and avoided. All those emotions of stored anger, insecurities, and our own childhood wounds. When the time comes for you to face your baby that is either screaming from the top of his lungs or constantly needs and physically demands your body through sucking, grabbing, biting, and pulling on you—that is where your unhealed parts come out and you finally face yourself, as you cannot run away any longer.

I grew up with a mother who loved me in her own way, but just didn't have the knowledge or the skills necessary to create a safe environment for me growing up. I was always longing for her unanswered love, well into my thirties. That has created so much anger and resentment in me, and I was so afraid I would transfer it to my son.

I wanted something different for my relationship with him. How would I raise him to become a confident, connected leader like this book states? I was very clear that he needed safety first. Deep love. Validation. Engagement. Presence. And playful fun.

I didn't know what that looked like, as it was never modeled for me! What does it look like in those uncomfortable situations when our child pushes our boundaries, says "no" to us, or even screams and hits us?

I grew up with authoritarian style parenting, where you have to do what adults tell you, "Or else!" Most of the time, it actually produced well-behaved kids in social settings, but they were also very traumatized.

What I saw, here in the United States, when I moved here was that parents have completely flipped the coin with their child-rearing techniques. They practice permissive style parenting. Since it's the opposite of my own, at first, it really attracted me and I was very curious about it. I want that gentleness with my son, and I want him to know that his needs matter, his voice is heard, and he is always loved and validated. With time, I started noticing something. A lot of the children I was observing are very self-centered and not empathetic to others' needs.

They say whatever they want, do whatever they want, scream, hit, manipulate, and have no repercussions for their actions. They always get what they want, but if they don't, God knows their parents will pay for it. It's almost like families have become child-centric and not parent-centric, like in the past. I am truly shocked by the level of disrespect children exhibit to both their parents and other adults around them. Will these kids become confident and connected? I highly doubt it. As a matter of fact, the mental health crisis is rampant now amongst American children and teenagers. Most are insecure, anxious, disconnected, and lack empathy.

In my opinion, neither of these two opposite sides of parenting truly work. Why am I saying all this in this *No-Problem Parenting* book? There are no simple tricks or rules about how to create a *confident* and *connected* child.

The way to this result is to do the work on *yourself* and lay a strong foundation with your child from the moment they are born.

What is this foundation made of? From my experience, it is made of:

1. Time being fully present and engaged with them.
2. Love, nurture, and affection.
3. Clear, effective, and nonreactive communication/boundaries.

If you have love and affection, but don't have clear boundaries and good, effective communication, your child will feel your love, but won't respect you. On the other hand, if you have effective communication and consequences, you aren't afraid to uphold, but rarely spend joyful, playful time with your children, they might listen to you, but they won't feel safe and happy to follow your lead. They might eventually rebel against you. The trick for us parents is we must do both.

We need to become confident leaders in order to confidently lead our children. If we are fearful, looking for love and validation from them and have our own anxieties about parenting, they will feel this and run with it. It is not because they are malicious, no. It is just a natural way for them to model their parents and sometimes, even exploit weaknesses and see what they can get away with. Children are looking for healthy boundaries, and if we don't give them healthy boundaries, they will feel very disturbed and chaotic.

Sometimes, confidence needs to be fake at first. Just like on a job interview or the first few days of a new project, we might feel shaky at first. But we have to "fake it till we make it." The same goes for kids. I am a huge proponent of authenticity, but when it comes to being a leader, we must actually practice these skills. Sometimes, in the beginning, they just don't feel natural to us.

Saying No

When we say no—we have to stick to it. No going back, no negotiating, and no minimizing our initial promise. No is no. For this reason, we should pick our battles very carefully and avoid saying no at all costs in the first few years of our kids' lives. They will ask us to do unreasonable stuff a thousand times a day, and those thousand times, we might want to say no, but we should try not to. Why? Because once you do say no and you experience resistance from your child, it will be extremely hard to stand your ground in the face of their tantrums and meltdowns. But you have to. If you want to earn their respect and establish healthy boundaries with them, you must keep your word.

Some ways to avoid saying no:

1. Redirecting.
2. Saying yes, but postponing the time.
3. Mirroring it back to them with consequences of two different actions they can take.

Giving Them Freedom

Children should be able to roam around freely and learn from the natural consequences and mistakes they make. We must encourage their childlike curiosity and creativity, not stifle it.

If we keep stopping every step that we might deem dangerous for them, we will make them fearful and anxious to even try. That difficult ladder-type structure on the playground—let them do it. That glass of water that they seem too clumsy to hold—let them do it. That mandarin that they don't know how to peel—let them do it.

Always ensure them, of course, for their safety, but do not interfere unless their life or health is at risk. Stop saying, "Be careful," all the time. Help them build their confidence instead of inadvertently tearing it down with your constant remarks and little unintended criticisms. You might not mean it; you might think you are just trying to care for and protect your child. The truth is you must let go. Like a bird that throws her little offspring off the nest, you need to let go energetically and allow them to come into their full-blown power. And it starts early. It starts with the first steps they take and even prior to that.

We must learn to trust our children. There is a whole movement of *baby led weaning* I have found and followed and highly recommend. From the time my son, Noah, was a baby, literally, since he was one-year-old or even younger, I have allowed him to hold objects, eat full apples without me slicing them or mashing them for him. I encouraged him to peel his own fruits, drink out of real glasses, help me to put real dishes away, help me with laundry, vacuum, allow him to wipe his own spills, allow him to learn how to dress and undress himself, brush his teeth, his hair, wash himself, go pee and poop by himself, and many more tasks, that most one, two or even three-year-olds don't do. I strongly believe all kids are capable of all of this or more, it is just that parents do not give them the opportunity or have enough patience or trust to allow the space for their kids to try this. When you go to third world countries and see these tiny kids that are so capable of so many tasks, it makes you wonder, are our kids any different? They are not, it is just the opportunities that we don't provide them. We'd rather keep them safe and shelter them, then empower them to learn and grow. How many three, four or even five years olds do we see still in strollers, when they are perfectly fine walking on their own? (This, of course, doesn't apply to special needs children, I understand that everyone's circumstances are different. I am talking about healthy children with no special needs.) I know there are exceptions to everything I am saying, but I am just trying to point something out that paints an overall picture of how our western civilization, in general, raises children. So again - we must trust our children and enable, not disable, their growth and development.

Presence and Engagement

Nothing you will ever do can replace being fully present, conscious, and engaged with your child.

It is the absolutely most important part of building healthy, secure, and confident kids. It is very hard to uphold any boundaries and increase their self-esteem without first creating a foundation of secure attachment and filling their cup with love.

What a gift that is for our children!

How many of us have grown up with the saying, “Children should be seen and not heard?” How many of us have been maybe taken care of physically, but our emotional needs went unmet, causing havoc in our adult relationships? How many of us would love to have received the gift of loving, present parents?

There is absolutely nothing more important than that for a child. Once your child’s cup is filled with your love, attention, and nurture, they can feel free and secure to roam and explore the world around them.

What does it look like to be *engaged* with your child? One of the examples of being engaged is very simple - maintaining eye contact.

We don’t just watch our child’s moves; we actually *connect* with them at eye level as many times as possible. We look at them; we truly see them. Who are they? We use curiosity and wonder to see them and be open to what unfolds in front of us. We don’t think of the next thing and what they are doing right or wrong, or the pile of laundry we need to do that is waiting for us. We stay in the *now* with them.

Communicate With Them, Not at Them

We ask them direct questions. We allow them the time to respond. We answer *their* questions, no matter how repetitive or crazy they are. We explain things to them. We don't just disregard them because they're blabbing away. Everything your kids do is a bid for your attention. And if we ignore those bids, we ignore their desire and need to connect with us and learn. I absolutely do understand and can relate to this being so tiring and exhausting sometimes, especially for our already overwhelmed nervous systems. We just do our best. We remind ourselves how important it is, and we breathe, reset ourselves, and come back to ourselves and our children, often when we have left.

Play Time

We take our time to play with them every single day and as much as we are able to. Is it hard? Yes. Do we need to kill ourselves by doing this? No. But we really make an effort. Kids *love* play, and they connect and build confidence through play. Having their parents engage with them in fun play is the most fun thing for a kid, and they will bond with you and increase their love and affection for you, which in turn will make them want to listen to you even more. So it is all connected. No solid and, most importantly, emotionally *safe* discipline can be achieved without trust and connection. And play provides that for our children. They learn to trust us, have fun with us, and become teammates with us. This is the most bonding activity and will go an exceptionally long way in building a solid base for your relationship. When it is playtime, it is important to gently encourage our children to discover things on their own, explore their own ways of doing things, and learn to be patient with them instead of just giving them the solution or telling them what to do or not to do.

All in all, becoming a conscious, responsible, loving parent is one of the most impactful ways we can heal and change the world for the better. Because in doing so, not only do we heal ourselves, but we heal the future of our humanity.

Kay Chorna

Kay Chorna is a woman, a wife, a conscious mother, a real estate Broker in San Diego, a social butterfly, and so much more in between. On top of her full-time real estate business, Kay has been leading women's self-empowerment events for over a decade now, as well as creating transformational women's book clubs, mega networking events, women's self-love events, and accountability groups. Currently, her family is exploring world schooling adventures and helping other families thrive through various avenues, including real estate, online coaching, and events/retreats.

Connect with Kay at

https://khrystynachorna.wixsite.com/accountability.

CHAPTER 11

The Gift of Dishes

Kelly Flood

Once upon a time there was a woman who believed she knew exactly how she was going to be as a parent and a mother. You can imagine her dismay when, after all of her hard work in making that vision a reality, nothing turned out as she planned.

I have very fond memories from my summers as a child spent at my grandparents' cottage with the extended family. Most evenings, when the adults retired to the sunroom, the cousins were tasked with doing the dishes after dinner. The number of tea towel fights, giggles, and serious conversations about topics we couldn't yet share with our parents that occurred created lasting memories, all while doing the dishes.

It isn't a surprise, then, that I found the *gift of dishes* during one of the most tumultuous times in my life, when everything I knew about my life at the time fell apart.

Before I tell you more, I invite you to come with me for a moment as we wash some dishes. I know what you are thinking … um, this is a parenting book and I have enough of my own dishes waiting for me, why would I want to imagine washing dishes? Indulge me for a moment if you will.

If you are listening to these words, I suggest you close your eyes and let my words paint a picture. If you are reading them, your imagination will create the perfect scene for you. Here we go...

You are standing at your kitchen sink. You see the pile of dirty dishes on the counter. Turn on the tap and place your fingers in the running water as it flows to the exact right temperature. Now plug the drain. Next pick up the soap bottle and squeeze the softly scented soap into the running water. Swirl the soap around in the water as it fills up the sink. Let the water and the bubbles run down your hands. Fill the sink with the dishes. Pick up a plate. Run the soapy cloth over the top and bottom of the plate. Watch the water and bubbles wash away the debris. Take the time to enjoy the flow of the clean, warm water on your hands as you rinse the bubbles off the dish and place it in the drying rack. Do this on repeat until all of the dishes are clean and placed in the drying rack, your hands are dried, and the sink is wiped clean. Stand back and appreciate a job well done. Now let's review the scenario from the beginning. Pay attention to how your body felt when you first pictured the pile of dirty dishes. Now notice how your body feels with all of the clean dishes drying in the rack. Are your shoulders less tense? Is your breathing slower? Are you breathing more deeply? Did you notice that your racing thoughts slowed down or quieted or disappeared while you washed the dishes?

Sensory regulation, the ability to monitor and control one's own feelings, emotions, and behaviours, is an integral part of being human. Knowing and understanding our own sensory regulation gives us insight into how we operate on a day-to-day basis. Water has an incredible effect on our body senses and regulatory system. I have learned that using water in any manner helps to create calm for me. Specifically, washing the dishes is a very centering, grounding, and calming activity. It offers me an opportunity to pause, check in with my mood, review my day, be curious about my emotional state, daydream and just let my mind rest. Symbolically, it washes away the debris of the day.

Co-regulation is how one person's nervous system influences another. For example, when an adult, who is able to be calm in the presence of a highly emotionally responsive child, the child is able to borrow that calm to manage their own sensory regulation in that moment. Therefore, knowing and understanding our own sensory regulation needs impact how we show up when in a situation that may require co-regulation strategies.

So here is how washing the dishes; sensory regulation, and co-regulation played a major part in my parenting journey.

A few years ago, I was professionally in my jam. I worked on a school board as an itinerant Speech Language Pathologist (SLP). I had two part-time roles. One as a member of a specialty team and the other as a collegial mentor. I was the expert who teachers, parents and other SLPs called on to help them learn to use clear communication and behavioural strategies for children with complex learning profiles. I was the one with the easy to implement and practical answers.

Personally, my life was finally on track after a pretty icky divorce that I had been able to pick myself up from. Life was moving along swimmingly.

I did not anticipate **my whole life** falling to pieces. Yet, here I was again with every morning starting the same at 6:30 a.m. – exhausted – feeling like I had run a marathon before my feet hit the floor. All of the chaotic thoughts non-stop … "*I can't think straight; I can't make a decision; I just want to run away and hide; I am a horrible mother; why me? … make it ALL STOP, plllleeeeeaaaaasssse.*"

Due to a complete system re-organization at work, both roles that I had been working in and had existed for 10 years, were shut down. This drastic change required me to move to a new office location; work with a whole new caseload of schools and families, and no longer be a member of a team nor be a mentor to my colleagues, but rather, work autonomously. Although I was still working within my profession, every aspect of how I practiced it changed overnight.

At the exact same time that I was navigating this new way of working, my son, who had been living his life between his father's house and mine, announced his decision to live full time at his father's.

Just like that the bottom fell out of what I thought was a pretty stable life.

A few big identities that I used to describe me were no longer true. I no longer was a team member. I no longer was the mentor. I no longer was the expert.

I no longer was a mom.

In my chaotic mind, I believed all those statements to be true.

Since I was so deep in anger and grief, I didn't realize at the time how beneficial this work change and office move was for both me and my son.

I was fortunate, though, to have a lot of flexibility with my work schedule so I decided that we would have a standing lunch date on Thursdays. Now consider at this time that my son is in Grade seven. He is very angry. He would rather be hanging out with his buddies during lunch recess. He doesn't want anything to do with me, let alone be forced to have lunch with me ... BUT his mom can't let him go just yet.

My new office location, which had a fully functioning kitchen, was literally at the bottom of the hill from my son's school. Therefore, I took advantage of that space and on Thursdays I brought lunch to work that we could prepare and eat together; and then clean up together.

Slowly a new ritual was created – every Thursday, the lunch bell would ring, and my son would come down the hill to my office. When he arrived, he was welcomed by my office colleagues (he loved that attention as he walked through the building to the kitchen). We then prepared our meal together. We ate together. We did the dishes together.

We did the dishes together.

Sometimes he washed and I dried, sometimes I washed, and he dried.

We did the dishes together.

The dishes. ... That sensory regulation activity, that very centering; grounding and calming activity that literally and figuratively washes away the debris. A co-regulating activity that created calm in me, the adult so that my son could borrow that calm for a brief moment. An opportunity each week for a fresh new start.

We did the dishes together.

I won't say it was all butterflies and rainbows every Thursday. There were some lunches that were just eat and run. Some were filled with angst and high emotions. Others were breezier and fun.

What I can only see with hindsight, what I now call KINDSIGHT, is that as a result of this new physical work location, my new work identity was being transformed at the same time as my new mom identity was being transformed.

Enter Human Design. Often called *the new astrology*, Human Design gives:

You specific information about your life path, your style of working, your relationship blueprint, how you experience energy in the world and most importantly, how to create a truly meaningful and authentic life.[1] ~ Karen Curry Parker

---

It also:

Teaches you how to honor and express your feelings so you are never a victim of emotional pain and suffering again.[2] ~ Karen Curry Parker

---

Ultimately, Human Design helps you discover your own unique energy and how to work with it in alignment with who you are meant to be. Ra Uru Hu, to whom this system was transmitted in 1987 during a mystical experience said, "it is for the children" and that resonates deeply with me.

If only I could have known this years ago, I would have most likely taken fewer things personally and would have also navigated other situations with more grace. Via Kindsight, I can see how Human Design would have helped me to understand my son differently.

I can only imagine that if I had known, through Human Design, that my son is here to live life through a trial-and-error type of experience, our relationship would have flourished earlier. Oh, all of the different ways I could have supported him through those formative years. What I could have shared with him about who he is and how his energy works, he may have navigated life differently when his social circles were in chaos. What I could have said differently to him when he literally physically broke and couldn't walk for six weeks and was restricted to a wheelchair and moved in with me full time for those six weeks after living full time with his dad. That experience is a whole other chapter I could write about! With what I know now about my own design and my son's design, some of our life experiences may have been less intense.

I learned that my own profile is driven to heal the world through powerful leadership while offering up practical solutions (cue my work role) and at the same time I require a significant amount of safety and stability. In Kindsight, I now see that Thursday lunches and the gift of dishes provided that safety and stability, both professionally and personally.

My relationship with my son has grown exponentially since Human Design arrived in my life. I understand him on a very different level and can now be his guide, or as Amy Ruth, Human Design expert states, *a chaperone*, for him. I am able to step back and honor his trial-and-error approaches to life. I am able to observe his up and down moods and not feel responsible for his emotional state. I know how to not take those emotions personally. I am his champion.

I believe that parenting is one of the biggest healing modalities and a place where practical solutions are needed. The impact of Human Design arrived later in my parenting journey. I want for you to have this awareness right from the beginning of your parenting journey as you chaperone your own children into this big wide world. I want for you to experience the gift of dishes in your own way and that is why I am here for you!

Once upon a time there was a woman who believed she knew exactly how she was going to be as a parent and a mother. You can imagine her dismay when, after all of her hard work in making that vision a reality, nothing turned out as she planned. In fact, it turned out even better.

[1]Introduction to Quantum Human Design, Karen Curry Parker

[2]Understanding Human Design; Karen Curry Parker

Kelly Flood

Kelly brings a unique lens to her new role as a Human Design parenting coach with close to 30 years experience working as a Speech Language Pathologist supporting families, children, and educators.

Call on her for the practical solution and if she doesn't have it you can bet, she will connect you to someone who does! A creative problem solver, Kelly will work with you using empathy and encouragement - she is your biggest fan when you succeed and is on the sidelines cheering you on when life pulls you a little off course.

When Kelly is not engaged in professional work you can find her walking in nature with her dog, having fun taking photographs; baking new treats in the kitchen; engaged in Board volunteer work with the local Community Food Pantry; gathering with friends and family to celebrate life and always cheering on her son as he embarks on 'adulting' life!

Connect with Kelly at

https://www.instagram.com/miss_kelly_flood/.

CHAPTER 12

From Uncertainty to Clarity: Breaking the Mold of Traditional Education

Kimberly Gawne

I never really comprehended why I didn't belong. Not until high school, that is. Even then, I was just barely starting to scratch the surface.

After the rough-and-tumble start – which I'll get to in just a minute, I promise – to what would be my short-lived private school experience, it was smooth sailing until I transitioned to public school. That was a nightmare, and a huge culture shock. Public school, with the curse words, the jeering attitudes, and the mean kids – it was not a pleasant time. And after what had been a very positive, albeit somewhat sheltered, experience in a Christian private school, I had a lot of adjusting to do. But I did it. Somehow I made it through the bullies in middle school and the isolation in high school. When I moved to university and teacher's college, I quickly became known through the entire campus as *the girl who disagreed with everything*. But let me back up a few years. Best to start at the beginning, right?

I am the oldest of three children, and was raised in a Christian home. My parents taught us all respect for others, while my father taught us to ask questions about absolutely everything, to insist upon uncomfortable conversations, no matter how unfortunate the timing might be. We were taught to respect others as people, individuals, and God's creation, but also to challenge ideas and concepts, and to let no stone go unturned in the search for the truth of the matter. While this sort of mentality didn't start to develop in any seriousness until I was much older, I was always told I was going to big places. One thing I always knew was that my parents believed in me.

This unshakable faith was only exacerbated at the age of 5, after I had a benign cancerous brain tumor, the size of a tangerine, removed. It was at the back of my brain, pushing on my cerebellum. My kindergarten teacher raised the alarm to my parents, when I had collapsed to the floor from an upright position.

My parents took me to our family doctor, and she suggested I be taken to the nearest pediatric hospital. There, tests were run and the discovery was made. I needed surgery right away, or I had a matter of weeks to live. At the time, medical equipment was not as advanced as it is now; this was almost 25 years ago, as of the publication of this book. My parents were told I had a 60/40 chance of being a vegetable, or seriously mentally impaired, if I lived. I don't remember the surgery itself, or very much before that, but I very vividly recall the hospital. Or, rather, I remember the experience of the hospital, both the lovely and the ugly. The needles, the MRIs, CAT scans, and resulting tears and trauma. I remember the Tim Hortons visits, and the footprints on the floor that traced their way throughout the entire hospital – painted there by, no doubt, a team of well-meaning janitors.

The most important thing I remember, and the best part of my detested follow-up visits. The neurosurgeon who had operated on me came to see me even just for 10 minutes, to ask how I was, to make the required physiotherapy demonstrations into a game. He'd hop up on the table himself, swing me up there, and proceed to gamify my reflex testing. Dr. James Rutka, of the Hospital For Sick Kids in Toronto. He couldn't make it every year, but he made more than he missed. I recently reached out and reconnected with him, and wouldn't you know it? He remembered me too.

My surgery and recovery, both physical and mental, ate up most of my two school years in kindergarten. No matter though – I was reading (again) in a matter of months after that. I entered first grade a happy, healthy, and by all accounts normal, child.

The rest of my elementary school year passed by fairly unremarkably, until I made the move to public school when I entered grade 6. That was a year of adjustment. I remember clear as day when I heard my first swear word, on the first day at recess, when I was out playing by myself. Although I'd never heard it before, I instinctively knew that it was a word that should not be said. I told the boy this, and asked him if *he wouldn't mind using nice words to express himself instead*. I got punched in the face for my efforts, and that set the tone for the year.

I learned how to defend myself with words. My parents taught all three of us children that violence was a last resort, and not something to be taken lightly. The remainder of middle school was not easy, grades 7 and 8 only got worse, and grade 8 culminated in the police being dragged into a cyberbullying incident in which I was the victim.

High school was the bane of my existence, for almost the entirety of my stay there. I focused on learning as much as I could. You could have locked me in the library and given me bread and water, and I would have been happy. I reveled in knowledge, and my father encouraged this in a variety of ways that I remain grateful for to this day. I had friends who I could eat lunch with and hang out with, but they were few and far between. Suffice it to say, I buried myself in reading and in work. I was working from the age of 16, in various positions, but mostly in educational fields of one sort or another, saving for university and teacher's college. I wanted to be a teacher. My father is yet again responsible for this; he was and still is an alternative educator, and remains the inspiration for a lot of my teaching philosophy.

I finished high school with a few International Baccalaureate certificates in English, History, and Music. I took the advanced courses, because I wanted to learn, and challenge myself.

Once I finished high school, it was off to university. That was where I put my debate and critical thinking skills to good use. I made fast friends with my professors; my classmates knew me as a brainiac, speed reader, and an alternative thinker. I cannot count how many debates professors had to break up between myself and other students. I was always the student with the answer, opinion, or suggestion. I couldn't help it – I loved to learn, and I genuinely could not understand why others did not feel the same way. Here, I scrambled to find my footing. I wanted to be respectful to others and explore presuppositions from both sides without sacrificing the truth. Of course, that typically was too sensitive of a topic for young adults to manage; I offended a great many people in the search to explore, trying to facilitate discussion and engagement.

Teacher's college was much the same, but with a smaller, more elite crowd. By the time I graduated with my degree, in April of 2020, I knew that I simply did not belong in the public education system. But here I was, sitting on two degrees – one a B.A., the other a B.Ed. – and I had no idea what I was going to do with them.

Hi! My name is Kimberly. I'm glad you've read this far. I am a passionate lifelong learner, teacher, and the founder of Star Students. That's my education story, and although it's been turbulent, frustrating, and often painful, it's paved the way for my career and that of others.

March of 2020 saw a massive change. A huge shift. As a new graduate, I started out offering tutoring services on my own, while I decided what to do.

Things quickly started falling into place. Tutoring exploded, as the value of a trained teacher who was willing and *happy to teach* rose steadily. By the second half of 2020, I was working on a contract as a private teacher. By late 2021, with the sort of messaging I had been putting out on social media, I was being approached by a variety of parents who were asking for homeschooling services. Something in my brain just ... clicked. This. This was how I was meant to serve, how I was destined to show up. It all made sense – everything I'd been through up until that point in my life had been preparing me for that privilege, that responsibility of homeschooling.

You as a parent are looking forward, looking towards the best opportunities for your child and homeschooling is an option. Let me dispel some common myths about homeschooling. The following list is intended to give you peace of mind.

1. I can't instruct my children; I'm not a teacher.

Whether you know it or not, you have been teaching your child since they were born (or placed in your care). They learn something from you every day, whether it be a certain vocal inflection, a facial expression, a new word, or a new life skill. There is nothing that you cannot unintentionally channel into learning experiences, rather than always using purposeful, planned lessons.

Now to be fair: if the above paragraph had you rolling your eyes (I know there's no university degree for facial expressions), I do realize that there will be subjects where you will need some outside help. This is where building a community of like-minded people comes in. The support, advice, and resources you will find in that community will help you acquire the information you need so that your child will be taught correctly when it comes to those more difficult academic subjects.

Don't forget to do your research! Read the books and articles, ask the questions, do the digging that is required for you to make a strong action plan for how you are going to educate the children in your care.

2. I don't have time.

Homeschooling does not have to be a six-to-seven-hour school day. Homeschooling can be conducted in two or three days per week, or a full five-day workweek. The following is a general guideline to the average amount of focused school time needed for each grade level, if you are following the traditional school curriculum:

Typically, 30 minutes per day is enough for children up to grade 1

Grade 1-2 requires 1 hour of focused study daily

Grade 3-4 requires 1.5 hours of focused study daily

Grade 5-6 requires 2 hours of focused study daily

Grade 7 and up requires a maximum of 2.5 hours of focused study daily

Makes you wonder why the days are dragged out to such an extent in traditional schools, doesn't it?

3. My kids will fall behind academically.

This myth comes from comparing homeschooling schedules to the full-day routine of traditional school systems. The fact is that children do not learn for six hours straight in school. If you find that there is a real concern with your child regarding the lack of academic knowledge, enlist some professional help. A tutor or teacher will be able to support your goals and bring your child up to speed if they are behind.

Remember that not all learning is linear; children develop in different states. Don't stress about them performing to a certain level. Continue to be patient and intentional in your teaching; your child will learn when they are ready.

4. I don't know what to teach.

If the idea of a free-flowing curriculum makes you nervous, there are plenty of other curricula that have been designed to mimic the traditional education system. As mentioned before, professional guidance is always available.

You don't have to be alone in this endeavor. If you need motivation, new ideas or creative methods, try going on to YouTube and searching *A Day in the Life* for homeschooling parents. There is a ton of content out there that will help reinforce the fact that there are many, many parents and caregivers who are choosing homeschooling as a way to give their children a meaningful and purposeful education.

5. My kids won't be socialized.

This one always makes me chuckle. In public school, your children are not trained to socialize, but instead to follow orders. They are told to sit down, be quiet, do this activity or worksheet, ask for permission to leave for water, etcetera. Public school is not the ideal place for socialization – outdoors and in a natural environment, learning or otherwise, is!

These are just some of the most common objections I've heard over the past few years, and these have always been my responses. A gradual shift towards natural learning is already happening in places around the world. As the shift continues, it is going to crescendo into a wave. That wave will eventually furl in, providing a clear and direct pathway through. But for now, being a crucial part of that crescendo is enough.

Kimberly Gawne

Kimberly Gawne is a passionate and dedicated educator with a drive to not only do things differently, but to do them better. She strives to bring a different perspective on current issues, particularly within the educational realm, and she has built Star Students around this model.

In her spare time, Kimberly loves to read mystery, adventure, and thriller novels. Baking is one of her favorite activities; she's got a cookbook full of old-fashioned and delicious recipes that she's collected since moving out West. She makes it a regular habit to stay active and fit; she would say she has to, because she loves creating or tweaking dessert recipes in the kitchen.

Kimberly is a first-time dog owner of two Cane Corsos named Tank and Rocksea, and lives on an off-grid homestead with her husband and many animals in the wild mountains of British Columbia.

Connect with Kimberly at www.starstudents.co.

CHAPTER 13

No Problem Rebounding Your Kids from Lockdown Learning Loss

Supporting Your Child's Academic Success Holistically

Kohila Sivas

As we move towards a post-pandemic era, it's clear that our children's overall well-being has taken a significant hit.

Although things are returning to normal, it's important to acknowledge that our kids are not the same as they were before the pandemic. What's particularly concerning is the massive learning loss resulting from the sudden shift that happened and the remote teaching and subsequent school closures.

Many of them are now facing the daunting reality of being two to three, or even more, years behind in their grade level.

I know this to be true because I work with students every day.

I'm an ex-teacher and a reformed tutor, I've dedicated my life to helping students succeed in school and beyond.

As a parent and teacher, I've witnessed firsthand the challenges that children face in the educational system. When I left the classroom many years ago, I did so because I wanted to help bridge the gap between what students needed to learn and what traditional teaching methods offered.

As I focused to unlock each student's full potential, I refined and re-engineered my methodology to create a holistic approach that addresses the whole child; to support their personal growth and academic success.

Drawing on my 24 years of experience in education, combined with my personal struggles, and my own personal application of mathematics as a form of therapy, I was led to develop a unique coaching process.

This is how my revolutionary MathCodes Method and the Meta-Learning DeStress Method was created.

The Meta-Learning DeStress Method is not just a coaching methodology, it's a philosophy that inspires hope and promotes growth. As an advocate for children's academic and personal success, I'm committed to serving students, parents, and other educators.

And I am very concerned about Lockdown Learning Loss.

As I speak to more and more parents and teachers, it's clear that our kids are struggling, especially those who were already facing challenges prior to the lockdowns. As a parent, it can be disheartening to witness your child losing interest in learning and becoming unmotivated.

The Meta-Learning DeStress Method focuses on empowering children through behavioral changes, addressing social-emotional well-being, and supporting academic growth. By taking a holistic B.S.E.M whole child approach, we can help children rebound from lockdown learning loss and help them thrive in all areas of their lives.

So, where do you start, and how can you help your child?

Here is what's important for your child's learning loss rebound:

Take a holistic B.S.E.M whole child approach to support your child's personal and academic success.

B. stands for Behavioral changes: Which is often the first sign that your child may be struggling in school. As parents, it's understandable to feel concerned when you notice these behaviors in your child. However, it's important to avoid lecturing or punishing them.

Instead, collaborate with your child and involve them in the process of addressing their challenging behaviors. Work together to identify the underlying causes of the behavior and come up with solutions to address them. This can help your child feel empowered and invested in the process, rather than feeling like they are being told what to do.

Communicate openly and honestly, approaching the situation with care and understanding. Ask them about their feelings and experiences and listen without interruption. This can help build trust and understanding between you and your child.

S.E. stands for their Social-Emotional well-being: Which can have a direct impact on your child's academic performance. The pandemic has had a significant impact on our children's social-emotional well-being

As parents, it's important to create a safe and supportive home environment where your child feels comfortable talking about their feelings. Encourage them to express their concerns or fears and listen without judgment or criticism. Reinforce the importance of self-care and encourage your child to prioritize their physical and emotional well-being. Try to put yourself in your child's shoes and understand their perspective. This can help you better support and empathize with them.

M. stands for Marks: Falling grades and poor test scores are some of the most obvious signs that your child may be falling behind in school. In my experience, when you address the B.S.E first, M always follows naturally.

If you notice your child's grades or test scores declining, the first step is to talk to your child and then to their teacher. They may have valuable insights into what's causing the issue and can provide suggestions for how to support your child at home.

You can also work with your child to develop a study schedule and encourage them to seek help from their teacher. Encouraging your child to take frequent breaks and offering positive reinforcement when they complete their homework can also help them stay motivated and engaged. It's important to celebrate their successes, no matter how small, and to recognize their efforts.

If you notice that your child is consistently struggling with homework, it may be a sign that they need additional support. Reach out to their teacher. It's important to address the B.S.E.M. factors first before seeking outside help, as this can help your child develop the necessary skills and confidence to succeed on their own.

As a former tutor myself, I know how tutors approach their work. I can tell you that tutors are not equipped to deal with the B.S.E.M. factors or address the root cause of the falling grades. Finding a tutor to address the falling grades, leaves the B.S.E.M. factors out the equation. Tutors will create dependency, and your child will gain false confidence.

To really help your child become an independent learner, B.S.E.M. must be addressed in the right order. Rebounding your kids from lockdown learning loss requires a holistic approach not a tutor's quick fix or band-aid solution.

Learning loss can be reversed, but it's critical to take the whole child approach.

Remember to be patient, understanding, and supportive as your child navigates the challenges of a post-pandemic world. It's important to remember that our kids are not the same as they were pre-pandemic, and it may take time for them to catch up academically. But with patience, understanding, and the right support, we can help our children rebound and achieve their academic goals.

If you want to gain more clarity, book a free Clarity Coaching Call with one of our certified Learning Success Coaches. We can support you and your child through this difficult time. Together, we can create a plan that works best for your child's learning style and helps them achieve their academic goals.

So, don't lose hope. As parents, we can be the catalyst for our children's success. By working together with our children and utilizing the right tools and resources, we can help them rebound from the learning loss caused by the pandemic.

Remember that our children are resilient and capable of great things. And with the right support, they can reach their full potential and succeed in all areas of their lives. So, let's take a deep breath, roll up our sleeves, and embark on this journey together. The future is bright, and our children's success is within reach.

Kohila Sivas

Kohila Sivas is a dedicated professional who has made it her life's mission to help educators, students, and businesses achieve success. She is the creator of the MathCodes Method™ and Meta-Learning DeStress Method™, unique systems designed to recover learning loss and demystify learning. The methods are grounded in brain science and neurolinguistics and help stressed-out learners destress themselves by talking to their brains and teaching them how to learn to learn. Our proven holistic coaching methodology is a unique and superior alternative to tutoring and teaching in all subjects. She is also the founder of Learning Success Coaches, she specializes in empowering educators by providing them with the skills, knowledge, and confidence they need to enhance student learning outcomes and run their own successful coaching practice. Kohila's expertise doesn't end with education. She is also the driving force behind Holistic AI Marketing, a cutting-edge business that offers comprehensive holistic business coaching and digital marketing solutions to businesses of all sizes.

Connect with Kohila at

https://www.learningsuccessacademy.com./.

CHAPTER 14

Five Steps to Lower Conflict in Family Communication

Mardi Winder-Adams

Most people assume that my interest in conflict resolution stems from living in a home with a lot of conflict. That in fact, couldn't be farther from the truth. My parents did not always agree, but always spoke with compassion and caring for the other person. I always assumed that most other human interactions followed the same process.

Needless to say, I did not hold that opinion for long, particularly when I started seeing how conflict occurred in other households. I saw conflict patterns emerge in friendships, dating relationships, and the workplace, and I experienced elevated levels of conflict and communication problems during my divorce.

This led to my fascination with conflict resolution. I became a mediator, behavior consultant, and divorce coach. I took courses and trained in managing conflict and creating environments that encourage the exchange of ideas, even in emotionally charged situations. I strongly believe that talking about conflict as a part of human behavior, not as a bad thing, is the first step in building skills and becoming a better communicator.

Parents can role-model the right way to disagree. You can change your behavior and move from high conflict to effective communication. Sometimes, the first step is determining how you define conflict and react when facing someone with a different opinion, idea, belief, value, or concern.

Some Basic Ideas About Conflict

Not all conflict is damaging to a relationship. In reality, positive change can occur only when there are disagreements about the status quo and dissatisfaction with how things are. When handled correctly, disagreements or conflicts are healthy and necessary to move any relationship forward. By encouraging healthy dialogue, new ideas, and differences of opinion in a productive way, communication becomes more interesting, innovative, and authentic.

At the same time, unresolved, ignored, or unhealthy types of conflict are destructive to a relationship. Months and years of unaddressed or unexpressed dissatisfaction lead to increased levels of chronic dislike and distrust. When families don't address these issues and sweep them under the rug, they can become a tinderbox waiting to ignite. It also leads to people not feeling valued or important in the family, further creating a divide.

There are effective conflict resolution and conflict reduction strategies to use in any situation. The more families use these strategies, the lower the level of conflict. The good news is that even one person using these strategies effectively reduces non-productive, angry, hostile, and damaging communication.

Constructive resolution of conflict is also applicable in business and other interpersonal interactions. These methods take practice, but once you internalize these strategies, you will notice a decrease in your reaction to conflict and an increase in more effective communication.

Let's look at five steps or strategies parents can use in difficult or challenging communication. These are also strategies parents can teach children, and kids can use in their conversations with friends, parents, and each other.

1. Know What You Want to Say

One of the most common mistakes people make is not identifying what they want to accomplish in a conversation. They know they don't like something or are not happy about an issue, but they fail to take the time to fully understand what is making them unhappy, uncomfortable, or angry.

Not having a clear agenda for a conversation allows things to get off-track very quickly. Rather than focusing on the outcome you want, you are more likely to be triggered into reacting to a verbal jab thrown by the other person.

If we are honest, we know how to push everyone in the family's buttons, and they know your triggers or hot buttons. If they want to derail a conversation, they simply push that button. This causes you to react, which takes the conversation off in another direction.

- Pick an issue, but only one – having one problem to discuss keeps the conversation on track. It also means the conversation can be handled in a reasonable amount of time. Issues have to be specific and clearly identifiable to avoid confusion. Talking about getting homework done before six o'clock is a specific issue. Starting the conversation with *no one ever does their homework* creates conflict.
- Say what you mean – using the *nicest* terms to describe what you want to say only leads to ambiguity and confusion. If you need to

talk about dirty clothes left on the floor, use that specific issue and not something like *how we can work together to keep the house clean.*

- Use facts, not judgments – it is very common to pass judgment on others, particularly those we know all too well. Avoid making judgment calls on their behavior and focus on the facts. In the example above, stating that *dirty clothes are left on the floor* is much less likely to cause conflict than a statement like *you don't care about how hard I work and how this house looks; it obviously doesn't matter to you at all.*

2. Choose Your Words Carefully

The old saying, *Sticks and stones may break my bones, but words can never hurt me,* is not just incorrect but completely wrong. Words have the power to cause long-lasting pain, loss of relationships, loss of self-worth, and loss of a loving family long after the slights and transgressions are uttered in anger.

In relationships, particularly in families, choosing words carefully is critical to avoid escalating a situation. When people have lived together or been together for years, they know the words and the non-verbal expressions that trigger anger, frustration, embarrassment, or even humiliation.

While it is easy to use this insider knowledge to get to the other person, it is only going to generate and escalate the conflict. People in conflict are unlikely to agree on a solution, even if it is a reasonable option. In fact, being in conflict and in a negative emotional state creates a mindset of adversity rather than collaboration.

3. Avoid Absolutes

Words that denote an absolute statement will result in the other person taking a defensive stance. They come across as blaming or judging, and they ramp up the anger and conflict rather than cool it off.

Two examples of absolute words are *always* and *never*. Instead of using these words, consider alternatives.

Instead of saying: You never support my role as a parent.

Consider saying: I would like to have support in this together as parents. What are some of the ways we can work together to send a consistent message to the kids about our expectations?

The result is a collaborative or problem-solving approach rather than defensiveness.

Other terms to avoid in a conflict include:

- You should have
- You never
- You always (with a negative or blame statement)

Of course, you also want to avoid saying you are always in the right, and they are always in the wrong!

4. Start with Listening

Most people do not listen to what the other person says if they are in a negative conversation or disagreement. Instead, they are listening for ways to prove the other person is wrong, providing incorrect information, or misstating the situation or the *facts*.

Listening is not a natural behavior in a disagreement. It takes practice and patience to train yourself to avoid the common mistake of talking over the other person. Jumping in, failing to acknowledge their message, and simply stating what you want make people feel unheard and valueless in the conversation.

There is a style of listening that is effective in being able to hear what the other person is saying. It is used by business professionals, coaches, therapists, and effective communicators to let the other person know they are heard. It also allows you to respond in a way that moves the conversation forward rather than in circles around blame and accusations.

Keys to Active Listening

The following are critical steps or keys to actively listening in any conversation:

- Don't assume you know what the other person is going to say next
- Don't assume you know the other person's thoughts or opinions until they are stated
- Listen without distractions (no cell phone, text messages, television, or computer interruptions)
- Listen for the tone of voice, the choice of words, and the emotion behind the words
- Avoid interrupting and allow the other person to finish completely
- Rephrase what they said by capturing the key components in one or two non-judgmental sentences, and ask if you have it right.
- Encourage the other person to tell you more to get a full understanding and prevent making assumptions

Here is a simple example of an active listening response to a request for a change in times to pick up the kids:

Coparent: I can't pick up the kids at four this week. I need it to be at five or six as I have to work overtime.

You: I hear you want to change the scheduled time for the pickup of the kids from 5 pm to 6 pm on Friday due to a change in your work schedule. Do I have that right?

Coparent: Yes, just for this week. I hope you can understand and make this change.

You: I have plans for 6 pm on Friday but this is important for the kids. Can we talk about a way for this to work out for us both?

This communication may initially feel strange, but it immediately puts both parents into problem-solving mode rather than blaming or shaming mode.

5. Collaborating Is Not a Dirty Word and Conflict Styles Do Matter

Unfortunately, in conflict, the thought of collaborating is seen as a weakness or a failure by the other person. Kids often see parents as the age-old *us against them* struggle, and admitting that Mom or Dad has a good idea is difficult at best. At the same time, couples in conflict may have problems recognizing the other person's idea is a good one.

Collaborating is very different than accommodating or compromising. Recognizing the difference between the three can help set up options for reducing conflict.

- Accommodating – giving into the other person's wishes, even if it is not in your best interests. Accommodating can be an option to consider when the inconvenience to you is limited, and it is not a battle you want to have over a minor or one-off type of situation. On the other hand, accommodating can leave you feeling like you aren't valued or weren't heard if this is your go-to approach.
- Competing – this is the more traditional win-at-all-costs approach to conflict. The problem with competing is there is a winner and a loser, and very little development of understanding in how to approach disagreements in the future more productively.

Competing ends communication and wears other people down until they give in. Over time, people stop trying to problem solve with competitive conflict style individuals.

- Compromising – comprising is a bit like splitting the difference. Neither person gets everything they want, but both get something they want from the agreement. Compromise is often a way to limit conflict and walk away with at least something rather than getting into a win-lose competition with the risk of escalating the problem or further damaging the relationship. For parents and kids, compromise can be a good starting point.
- Collaborating – this is the ideal conflict resolution style and strategy. In collaboration, everyone gets what they need to the degree that makes them feel satisfied with the solution. Collaboration often involves creative problem solving and thinking outside of the traditional way of resolving disputes, which means it takes time and practice.

Everyone in the family has some elements of these four styles. Talking about different ways to approach and resolve conflict in the family is always a great place to start.

Final Thoughts

Effective communication strategies include preparing for difficult conversations, taking breaks, looking for ways to collaborate, staying curious, and listening to other people rather than trying to prove your point.

Kids and parents can learn these techniques to develop communication skills even through difficult conversations. Parents can model conflict resolution for children in their interactions with each other and the kids. Families can also take time to have collaborative discussions and use problem solving when there are differences in the family.

Effective conflict resolution is a skill everyone in the family will benefit from practicing and using in daily interactions. Conflict resolution is also a skill needed in all aspects of life, from interpersonal relationships with loved ones and friends to the necessary skills to succeed in any professional role.

Mardi Winder-Adams

Mardi Winder-Adams is an ICF and BCC Executive and Leadership Coach, Certified Divorce Transition Coach, and a Credentialed Distinguished Mediator in Texas. She has worked with women in executive, entrepreneur, and leadership roles navigating personal, life, and professional transitions. Mardi is the founder of Positive Communication Systems, LLC.

Connect with Mardi at https://www.divorcecoach4women.com.

CHAPTER 15

No More Angry Dads ...

Dr. Mort Orman, M.D.

If you're a dad and you get angry at your spouse, your ex-spouse, or your kids more often than you'd like, I have a message for you. You don't have to keep getting angry. You don't have to keep having minor things (or even major things) irritate you, annoy you, or throw you into a full-tilt rage. You can tame those ugly anger urges inside you. You can learn how to turn them off whenever you want.

I'm not talking about anger management here. I'm not talking about punching a punching bag, or counting to 10, or taking some deep breaths before you decide how to best communicate your anger.

I'm talking about **not getting angry anymore** ... so you don't have any anger building up inside you that you need to communicate to anyone. I'm talking about you learning how to win against your anger. You, taking your anger on ... and beating it to a pulp. I'm talking about you knowing how to knock your anger to the mat so hard that it just lies there, inert, and totally defeated, not wanting to get up and mess with you again. You already have the power and ability to do this. You just don't know it.

The reason I can confidently say this is because I used to be an extremely angry guy, until my mid-30s, and I didn't know back then that I had this power, either. But I did, and the past 40 years of my life have been mostly free of anger. More on my own anger story later.

When you learn how to make your anger go away, without having to manage it, your life will be so much better. Your health will be better. Your blood pressure will be lower. Your immune system will be stronger. Your marriage will be more secure. Your spouse will be happier. And your kids will feel less threatened and traumatized by your angry disposition, or your angry outbursts directed at them.

Kids don't react well to anger from their parents. Their little brains don't understand, process, or forgive anger as easily as our adult brains do. They tend to take your anger as their parent, very personally. They tend to interpret each episode as if something is wrong with them, or that you don't really love them, or even worse, that they are not lovable to anyone. Your anger can cause real psychological damage and lasting harm to your kids. And this can impair their ability to be happy and emotionally stable as they grow up into adults.

So, we are talking about real danger here. Your anger is not innocuous. It's not the badge of leadership or righteousness you might think it to be. Anger can damage your health, damage your career, ruin your marriage, and harm your kids. I assume you don't really want to cause any of these things. But, if you keep getting angry, and you never learn how to free yourself from this quite common human problem, I'm afraid you are in store for some of these unwanted consequences.

What Can You Do?

After 40 years of collaborating with countless parents and non-parents, I have found that there are **three things** all of us need to know and understand about our anger:

- How to correctly understand what is causing it to occur?
- How to know, with certainty, what we can and can't control about it.
- How to make our anger quickly disappear whenever we want.

I have developed a successful 10-session training program in which I teach people how to do these three key things.

It's called **Angry No More** and if you have any anger issues at all, large or small, you should definitely check it out.

What's Really Causing You to Get Angry?

Now you may think you know exactly what is causing you to get angry. After all, it's pretty obvious. You can see it. Others can see it. People doing stupid things. People letting you down or disappointing you. People breaking promises or life-long vows. Your kids not behaving properly or defying your authority as their parent. People moving way too slowly. Traffic is not moving at all. Politicians doing evil things. Bureaucrats not being helpful. And then there is unexpected stuff like Covid. It's never ending. But it's also not the whole story about what is actually causing you to become angry.

You see, we've all been taught to assume that anger is a two-step process. Something happens that obviously looks bad or wrong (Step 1) and this directly causes anger to surge within our bodies (Step 2). The real truth is that anger is actually a **4-Step process**. Step 1 is when something happens that obviously looks bad or wrong. Step 4 is that you feel anger in your body. There are two other steps (Steps 2 and 3) that are completely invisible to you and to outside observers.

Without these two invisible steps, the emotion of anger would never occur. This also explains why two people can be exposed to the same external event and one will become terribly angry or even enraged, while the other one won't. These 2 invisible steps go on entirely within our bodies, and unless you've been trained to recognize and understand them, you will remain blind as a bat as to why your anger is actually occurring. This, unfortunately, is where most people are today. And you will be hopelessly unable to deal with your anger powerfully and successfully. This is also, unfortunately, where the vast majority of people are today as well.

One of the things I do in my 10-session training program is to teach people how to correctly understand what is causing their anger to occur. Once they know this, their anger elimination powers (already within them) become available to them to access. And they can bring these powers to the playing field, so they can start to defeat their anger each and every time it occurs.

What You Can and Can't Control

We all have been poorly trained to understand and control our emotions. If you don't believe this is true, just turn on your television (or scroll social media on your phone or tablet) and tune into any news channel. You'll see people easily losing their temper, shouting, and screaming at each other, being verbally abusive to one another, and even resorting to violent physical acts. The result of this poor education is that we don't understand our emotions or what we can and can't control about them.

For starters, you can't control most of the things outside of you that trigger your anger or any other emotion. Sometimes you can, and if you have this opportunity, run with it. But most of the time you can't totally control what your wife does, what your ex-wife (or wives) do, what your kids think, feel, or do, what lawyers do, what judges decide, or who wins local or national elections. You also can't control the weather, the stock market, or the flow of traffic on the roads where you live or travel.

Unfortunately, you can't control whether or not you get triggered to feel your emotions, either. You will get triggered. Your kids and your life-partners know how to trigger you. And they are not suddenly going to stop. Even when you learn how to accurately understand what exactly within you (specific thought patterns and behavior patterns) is really causing your anger to occur, this knowledge will not prevent your body from responding with anger each and every time it becomes triggered. Yes, over months and years you can successfully reprogram your body to stop being so overly reactive, but not right away. In the beginning, you are going to keep getting triggered for as long as it takes for this to stop.

What you CAN CONTROL however, is what you decide to do each and every time you get triggered to feel angry. There are skills you can easily learn that can put you in charge of your emotional responses … not the other way around.

There Are Only Two Ways to Deal with Anger …

Contrary to popular belief, there are not just two ways to deal with anger - suppress it or express it. I know this is what you've been told, but it's not really true. There is a third and even better way - to simply make your anger quickly disappear whenever you want, without any symptom-oriented anger management techniques.

This is the third thing I teach my clients how to do when they hire me to help them get rid of their long-standing anger issues.

Winner or Loser?

So now that you know there is a quick and easy way to learn how to completely reverse and defeat any anger issue you might have, what are you going to do? Are you going to keep losing and paying significant costs, in your battles and struggles with anger in your life? Or are you going to decide to finally become a winner?

I've favored winning most of my adult life, so that's what I recommend you decide to do. And I'd be honored to be your coach if you genuinely want to learn how to win. I know what it feels like to constantly lose against anger. I was overly angry and irritable in my 20s and early 30s. Even when I became a physician, I would get angry with my patients, if they didn't follow my advice, which was sometimes the case.

However, about 40 years ago, I discovered how to end my anger problems once and for all, and during the past 40 years, I have had little to no anger at all. Also, over the past four decades, I've taught many other people to accomplish the very same thing.

So, if you want to stop being the angry dad, you can. If you want to stop blowing up at your wife, your ex's, and your kids, you can. If you want to stop holding on to long-term hurts, disappointments, and resentments, you can. And if you want to stop getting angry at yourself, you can do that as well.

All it takes is two things:

YOU decide you want to become a winner.

YOU find a coach who can help you accomplish that goal … quickly, so you can get on with having a happier, healthier, and more peaceful life.

After reading this chapter, if you are a dad who has anger issues, you are going to decide to do something. Either you are going to decide that it's okay with you to keep losing your ongoing battles to control anger in your life, or you are going to decide that it's time for you stop putting up with or excusing your anger and learn how to become a winner.

Here's hoping you make the right choice for you, your spouse, and your kids.

Dr. Mort Orman, M.D.

Dr. Mort Orman, M.D. is an internal medicine physician with 40 years of success as an anger elimination expert. He is creator of the *Angry No More* 10-session quick anger mastery program, and he has led more than 100 anger and stress elimination workshops for doctors, nurses, lawyers, business owners, entrepreneurs, other professionals, and even the F.B.I. He has also been the official sponsor of National Stress Awareness Month in the U.S. every April since 1992.

Connect with Dr. Mort Orman, MD at http://TheAngerSolution.org.

CHAPTER 16

No Problem Co-Parenting: Child Centered Success Strategies During & Long After Divorce!

Rosalind Sedacca

Let's face it. Divorce is never pretty and it's never easy. Especially when kids are involved. Most parents find themselves riddled with guilt. Then there's confusion, anxiety, fear and an array of other emotions. It's only natural to feel that way. To want to *protect your innocent children from hurt, anger and long-term emotional scars.*

My own divorce took place many years ago. What I've learned became the foundation of my Child-Centered Divorce Network for parents. It's also why I became a Divorce & Co-Parenting Coach, author, podcast host and recognized worldwide as The Voice of Child-Centered Divorce!

My personal story has a happy conclusion. My son was eleven when we divorced. He grew up, became a successful professional, married and has blessed me with a precious grandchild, too. His Dad and I were both present at all our son's wonderful childhood occasions, the rewards of successful co-parenting.

I want your story to have a happy ending, as well. Because your children deserve it! Did we make mistakes? Absolutely! Over time my Wasband and I learned how to create a child-centered divorce. We put aside our differences and focused on what really mattered most – being the best parents we could be to our son.

It wasn't always easy. But it was successful! We learned a lot as we moved through those years: The mistakes we made. Pitfalls to avoid. Skills to master. How our child was affected by what we did, what we didn't do, and how we resolved it.

I've been coaching parents on divorce and co-parenting issues for more than fifteen years. I've learned what works and what doesn't. When to speak and when to bite your tongue. Communication skills that diffuse anger. How to date as a parent. Behaviors that will hurt your children by hurting your ex. The list goes on …

I want to share some of the most significant insights here. So, you start on the right track, during and after divorce, by putting your kids first.

Make Parent-Child Communication a Top Priority Through Divorce & Beyond

One of the biggest challenges parents face during and after divorce is having healthy communication with their children. All parents struggle with communication issues as their children grow. However, children whose lives are dramatically altered by divorce need even more attention and more diligent observation by their parents.

Children usually don't tell you when they are angry, confused, hurt, or depressed. Instead, they reflect their problems through their behavior. Often that means acting out or turning inward in ways you hadn't experienced prior to the divorce. That's why you must do all you can to encourage positive and productive communication with your children. It's easy to forget your child's need for bonding and attention amid the challenges you are juggling with in your own life on a daily basis. However, this is crucially important: Take time to see the world through your children's eyes before making any decisions. That process alone will help you to meet their needs more effectively. Equally important, you'll be better prepared to understand their confusion, sadness or aggression. That mindset will support you in finding appropriate ways to dissolve tension through your conversations and caring behaviors.

Here are some useful tips for improving your communication efforts

Be available and attentive when your child comes to talk or ask questions. Turn off the TV, put down the tablet, don't answer the phone. Greet them with eye-contact and a welcoming smile. Often, talking to you comes after considerable thought and risk on their part. Encourage these conversations when they happen. Try to sit, kneel and get down closer to your child's eye level when you talk. Towering over them can feel intimidating and not safe. Don't dismiss a subject if it's bothering your child. Laughing or teasing will create mistrust. Trivializing their feelings will discourage your child from sharing candidly with you. This is a dangerous road to travel, especially as your children develop into their teens.

Equally important: never embarrass your children or put them on the spot in front of others. This will close the door to honest, trustworthy communication.

Avoid talking when you are angry with them or upset with others. If you're not calm, suggest postponing it for an hour or two so you can settle down and regain your objectivity.

Be an active listener. Don't interrupt your child. Listen carefully and paraphrase back what you heard them say. Ask if your interpretation is correct. They'll tell you. This process will help you better understand what's really at issue.

Insights to Contemplate

Children who feel safe talking to their parents become better communicators overall. They'll likely have healthier communication in their own adult relationships with their love partners and children.

You can open the doors to improved communication by starting today. Your children may be a little resistant at first. But they will surely appreciate this opportunity once they know you are sincere. Start the process yourself and see how valuable it is to hear what your children have to say!

Six Ways to Boost Confidence & Connection with Your Kids After Divorce

Divorce is often a time for disconnect. It's not uncommon for you to feel alone, rejected and insecure in the months following your divorce. So can your children. It is important for you to strengthen your bond with your children during this time of transition – whether you are living with them or apart.

Children want to know they are still loved, valued and cared about. Show them, tell them and keep in close communication with them. That's equally important during the happy times as well as the sad ones. They want to know they have a safe place to turn, a shoulder to cry on and a non-judgmental ear when they need it. This is true even if you are not physically together.

If divorce has been tough on you remember it's even tougher on them. They may not say so or confide in you. But it's a reality they live with every day.

Bottom line: your children must feel connected with you, know they matter to you and are always important in your life whether they are near you or not!

Here are six meaningful ways you can reinforce confidence and connection with the children you love.

1. Connect through notes: If you're living together, slip a note in your child's lunch box or notebook every few days. A quick joke, cartoon, reminder about a special event ahead or just a warm I Love You! will let them know they're on your mind and in your heart. If you're not spending time together, send an email note or a quick text message to convey that you're thinking about them.

2. Connect through idle chats: Take advantage of idle moments when you're together with your child. Driving in the car is a great time to ask questions, share feelings, and be empathic about their comments. Strike up a conversation when helping them with homework, cooking meals together or doing other chores. Just be mindful not to turn these conversations into lectures. You're there to listen, reflect and learn. If you judge or condemn, you'll close the door to hearing any more.

3. Connect through technology: Explore video chats, age-appropriate apps, interactive messaging and the array of virtual games you can play at the same time. These create bonds despite distance. They also encourage future appointments to spend time together. Those activities give kids something significant to look forward to. The gift of your attention!

4. Connect through bedtime routine: It's always wise to create a before bedtime routine with your children that integrates warm connection. Spend time reading books. Talk about your own childhood memories and challenges. Share personal insecurities and how you overcame them. Ask about the best part of their day or a new lesson they learned, focusing on the positive. Bedtime routines help you both unwind and create a bond that most children value. This works even at a distance. A scheduled nightly text, phone or Facetime conversation can provide security and joy to a child.

5. Connect through a new project: After divorce many things change in a child's life. So, create connections through new projects that have special meaning. Whether it's a multi-day puzzle, a plastic model you complete together, or decorating projects in their bedroom, this shared time promotes conversations, listening to music and stress-free connections. Following a baking recipe in two different kitchens or building projects in two garages serves a similar purpose. Sending photos or videos of your works in progress provides the same sense of connection and continuity with one another, even at a distance.

6. Connect through scheduled dates: Occasionally create a special outing alone with just one of your children. Take them to lunch, the zoo, a shopping trip, sports game or wonderful movie. Children cherish alone time with you and the opportunity to catch up without competition from siblings. Prepare this date in advance so you both have something to look forward to. Take photos. End with a keepsake reminder of your time together. Be sure all siblings get their special time with you as well.

It doesn't take much to reinforce your connection with your children during and after divorce. It's the sincerity of your effort, not what you spend, that impacts their lives. Caring attention helps them feel confident, loved, and secure despite the changes and challenges created by the divorce. Make the time to keep connected with your kids. You won't regret it!

What Children of Divorce Wish Their Parents Knew & Understood!

Children of divorce belong to a unique club no one wants to join. They learn their parents are divorcing. Their lives suddenly change. FOREVER! All they can think about is: NOW WHAT?

Over time, children get the answers. Learn how to cope. Go on with life.

When asked what they wish their parents understood about being a child of divorce, these kids aren't shy. There's a consensus of simple advice they're eager to share with any adults who will listen.

Here's what your children want you to know that many divorcing and divorced parents don't know.

1. We don't want to know about your divorce drama and why you're fighting again. We just want you to stop!

Fighting around the children is emotionally damaging for all kids. It's just that much worse when divorced parents do it. Give your kids a break and keep your battles away from their eyes and ears at all times!

2. We often miss our other parent when we're at your house. Please don't give us grief about that.

Let your child talk about and contact their other parent when appropriate. Hopefully, your co-parent will show compassion by reciprocating. Children really appreciate it.

3. We know the divorce has been hard on you and we hate to see you sad. But it's painful when you make us your confidant or therapist.

Turning your child into your friend or confidant robs them of their childhood innocence. Let your kids be kids and not your parents! Find a professional to help you deal with your pain.

4. We don't love you less when loving our other parent and you should know that!

Children must feel free to love both parents and be loved by both parents. Co-parenting shouldn't be a competition. Don't guilt your children for doing what comes naturally.

5. We hate being asked about our other parents, their home or love life.

Kids notice many forms of exploitation and don't like it. Asking children to spy makes them extremely uncomfortable. They may lie, exaggerate, take sides, or purposely misguide you when they know this is your intention.

6. We're uncomfortable with new "friends" in your life so be patient. Don't expect instant happy endings.

It may be hard to hear, but it's true. Be mindful and compassionate when introducing your children to new relationship partners. Take your time, value their feedback, and make sure they understand no one will ever replace them in your heart!

One last thought. Remember, you're a role model for your children. So be the best, most loving, and responsible parent you can be. Be supportive and helpful. An attentive listener. Compassionate. Eager to share their good moments without jealousy. Happy when they're happy. Empathic and approachable when they're sad. And always connected.

Divorced or not, isn't that what parents are for?

Rosalind Sedacca

Rosalind Sedacca, CDC is recognized as The Voice of Child-Centered Divorce. She is a Divorce & Co-Parenting Coach and founder of the Child-Centered Divorce Network. Through her international network she provides support, coaching, online programs and other valuable resources for parents who are facing, moving through or transitioning beyond their divorce. Rosalind is a divorced parent herself. She understands the anxiety, guilt, anger, fear, frustration, and pain parents experience during and after divorce. She is the author of How Do I Tell the Kids About The Divorce? A Create-a-Storybook Guide To Preparing Your Children – With Love! a professionally acclaimed eBook designed to help parents get through the tough divorce talk with the best possible outcome for themselves and their children. Rosalind has also created several eBooks and e-courses on co-parenting success strategies including an 8-hr Anger Management For Co-Parents and Dating After Divorce programs for women and men. She also hosts the Divorce, Dating & Empowered Living Radio Show & Podcast. Rosalind's primary concern is helping her clients minimize any negative effects on all children — not only in the months ahead, but in the decades to follow, as well.

Connect with Rosalind at www.childcentereddivorce.com.

CHAPTER 17

Matters of Life and Death

Why Connecting Generations Through Family Stories Is More Important than Ever

Ruthanne Warnick

If you're reading this book, it's likely that you're a parent or grandparent. In either role, generations are on your mind, whether front and center or somewhere in the back.

The reality about generations is, in the most direct way to say it, they come and they go. Not in the easy-come-easy-go way, but in the cycle of life way. The gift of life comes with the pain of loss. There's no way around it.

In the cycle of life, sharing family stories about experiences, values, traditions, memories, and the lessons of life connects generations. They connect living generations with each other in the present, and they connect us with those who have passed on.

Whenever I bring up the topic of family legacy through family stories, the most common and immediate responses I hear over and over are about regret and longing. "I wish I had asked more questions." "I wish I knew more about my grandparents." I hear the longing of wanting to stay connected with those they have lost or those they have never even met. People regret that they weren't more intentional about capturing the stories and asking the questions. I've had that longing and regret myself, and you probably have, too.

"May their memory be a blessing." ~Zichronam l'vracha

This is a Hebrew expression used when referring to someone who has passed away, and it's meant to honor that person and to comfort the bereaved. It says that their life mattered and was a blessing to others, and that we hope it will continue to be a blessing. After a couple of generations, though, when those who knew them are no longer alive, how do we continue to make their memory and their lives a blessing? How can we make sure their stories, and our own, don't disappear?

My father passed away when I was 40. It wasn't until years later that I realized how many stories died with him – about his own life, his immigrant parents' lives, our relatives who were killed during the Holocaust, and so much more. Years later, I came across a letter I had saved and tucked away. It was a letter my father wrote and shared with me shortly before I got married – a letter from father to daughter. It included some gems about what makes a marriage work and his wishes for me and my soon-to-be husband. Reading that letter after so many years was such a powerful and emotional experience - having his words and his voice in writing living on like that. Even now, whenever I read it, it's like he's sitting with me.

I had no idea how important all of this would become – the missing stories, the letter, and the yearning. I came to understand how easy it is for words to get lost over time, as the generations continue. If they aren't captured and shared with intention, living generations lose out on the benefits and future generations are essentially robbed of them. Instead of becoming family treasures, they become buried treasures – literally.

No doubt you have hundreds, if not thousands, of photos on your phone and other devices. It's likely you have boxes of photos from back in the day when film cameras were a thing and photos had to be developed. If you're lucky, you also have photos of past generations, some of which are labeled and some unfortunately not. All those pictures without the words, though, fall short. They don't have the stories. While the saying goes, "A picture is worth a thousand words," I say that "If a picture is worth a thousand words, a picture plus the words is priceless."

I started Capture the Journey to help families connect the generations through family stories and experiences and create treasured gifts of legacy. The importance of sharing family stories goes far beyond getting stories *for the record* before someone dies. That only focuses on the loss and death part, the one-way-street passing-down part. What about the life part? Through family stories, traditions, values, history, memories, and the lessons of life, you are able to connect the living generations of your family with each other, as well as with the past. It's like a woven tapestry, and we, the living, are the weavers.

What do our stories really represent? They share about struggles, overcoming adversity, and navigating challenges. They include successes and disappointments, history and heritage, values, traditions, and lessons learned along the way. In lighter ways, they share antics and humor, adventures, and misadventures, and back-in-the-day slices of life. They are all part of the tapestry, and they become part of our children's and grandchildren's stories, too.

Much has been written about the benefits of sharing family stories. They can provide guidance, strengthen bonds within the family, and provide a fundamental sense of belonging and emotional wellbeing. For older family members, taking interest in stories from their lives can help them feel that they are an important part of the family and that they matter. Think how meaningful all of that would be in your family. We often don't realize the impact those stories can have, even when it seems that someone's not listening. That's the thing about the stories. They're gifts we give and gifts we receive that we don't always recognize without a bow and giftwrap.

Here's the short version of a real-life, multi-generational story. When my husband Larry was ten, he and his father were at a Boy Scout meeting for prospective new members of the troop. The new scouts were asked to introduce themselves, and a boy named Raymond stood up to take his turn. The Scoutmaster then made a stunning comment. "We don't want your kind in this troop." The packed room fell silent. No one said a word. You see, Raymond was of Japanese descent, and this was in the 1960s when, sadly, anti-Japanese sentiment following World War II continued. Raymond and his father left the meeting humiliated.

Larry's father leaned over to him and said, "We're going with them. Raymond and his dad are our friends, and if they're not welcome here, we're not staying." They walked out and never returned. That one story is packed with lessons. It lets our children know about their grandfather's character and about doing the right thing even when it's not popular. It's a story of how, from a young age, Larry's values were formed and how he learned by example to view people individually and not judge them as part of an entire group. It's a three-generation story that doesn't just pass down a story. It connects and weaves together those three generations – with a bonus history lesson about the times, too.

After my maternal grandfather passed away, years before I was born, my grandmother moved in with us. She lived with us my entire life until I left for college at the age of 17. All those years, she lived right there, and we never talked about her life or about the grandfather I never knew. My paternal grandmother lived in the same town and passed away when I was nine. The memories are few. She and my grandfather on that side of the family were immigrants, and you can bet that I wish I had more stories. The importance of, benefits of, and ultimate loss of family stories just wasn't on anyone's radar at the time.

One day, I showed my son a photo of my mother. My parents had taken my siblings and me on a wonderful vacation for their 25th wedding anniversary. My mother was in her forties, and, in the photo, she is sitting on a chaise lounge on the beach, in a swimsuit, with her blonde hair down to her shoulders. I was chuckling about the funny look she had on her face, but he was struck by how young she looked. He blurted out, "Wow, I never thought of Grandma like that." To him, she was Grandma. It's sometimes difficult for children or grandchildren, no matter the age, to see us as more than a parent or grandparent. I knew then that I needed to share more stories.

In today's world, where so many family members live far apart and the family *village* is not what it once was, being intentional about sharing family stories is more challenging and more important than ever. The connections through family stories cannot be left to chance. Intention is the name of the game. Without it, we become more than just geographically distant.

As a parent or grandparent, you have the opportunity to be a family stories weaver no matter the age of your children or grandchildren and no matter how far apart you live. If you have living parents who are able, you have a double opportunity: to capture stories for the future before it's too late, and to weave together living generations in the present.

Three Keys to Being Intentional

Listen

Always be listening. Pay attention to all the opportunities to weave in a story about yourself, a parent, or a grandparent.

Listen for stories from family members, especially older ones. Some will be obvious stories, and others will be snippets mentioned in passing. For those latter ones, ask some questions that allow them to elaborate.

Share

Share stories relevant to children's current life stages and struggles, even when you think they're not listening.

For a younger child, relate a family story during story time.

Make stories part of conversations at the dinner table.

Use photos as memory joggers to get stories flowing.

Children of all ages can be family story weavers, too. Engage them, so they become part of the process. Consider creating a family project where everyone gets involved by adding stories and photos on an ongoing basis.

Record

On one hand, today's technology can make capturing stories easy. We can record with the touch of a finger. On the other hand, without being intentional, the technology doesn't matter.

Be ready to record impromptu stories on your smart phone or when you are screen-to-screen via Zoom, etc. Ask questions in a conversational way to get them to elaborate.

If a family member is willing, schedule a time or multiple sessions to ask questions about their life, family history or traditions, or memories of past generations. Consider it sacred time.

Keep a notebook to write down questions that you specifically want to ask, stories that you want to come back to another time for more details, and stories that you weren't able to record, i.e. you were in a noisy restaurant or driving in a car.

Remember to record your own stories, too.

Final Thoughts

The bottom line is to be intentional. Make it a priority. Otherwise, procrastination will win the day and the someday you were waiting for will never come.

While there are many ways to put your family stories together with photos, videos, and audio recordings, that's not the focus of this chapter. I would be remiss, however, if I did not mention **legacy letters** as a powerful and lasting way to share stories, wisdom, values, memories, and love. They convey the important things with intention and in a focused way that becomes a priceless treasure. The letter from my father that I mentioned earlier ended up becoming a kind of legacy letter, even though it was not his original intent. He shared it in the present, and more than 40 years later I still have it. There is not enough space in this chapter to elaborate, so please contact me directly to learn more about how you can create a *Legacy Letter of Life and Love.*

Now that you know the importance of sharing and capturing family stories, will you make it a priority? Will you be intentional? Will you avoid the regret of not getting around to it?

Don't it always seem to go that you don't know what you got 'til it's gone?

~Joni Mitchell, song Big Yellow Taxi

Although Joni was referring to paving paradise with a parking lot, the message applies here, too.

I titled this chapter Matters of Life and Death and started off with the cycle of life. Is all of this a matter of life and death in the urgent sense? No. No one is going to die if you don't share the stories. Is it a matter of life and death in the important sense. Yes, it is. How important is up to you.

Ruthanne Warnick

Ruthanne Warnick is a champion of the importance of sharing family stories, experiences, life lessons, and memories to connect generations. In today's world, with family members often spread apart, being intentional about capturing and sharing those stories is more challenging and more important than ever.

As a speaker and workshop facilitator, family legacy guide, and certified Guided Autobiography instructor, Ruthanne is committed to helping families take action, avoid regret, and connect living generations with each other and the past. Her passion for generational connection and legacy through family stories is fueled by her 32 years of non-profit leadership experience in the Jewish communities where she has lived, her own family stories and experiences, and her educational background with a master's degree in geography.

Ruthanne is the author of *Say It Now: The Important Things – A Guidebook for Creating Legacy Letters of Life to Celebrate Those You Love* and the creator of the *Legacy Letters of Life and Love* program.

Connect with Ruthanne at https://CapturetheJourney.com.

CHAPTER 18

No-Problem Parenting – Advocacy

Teresa Dawn Johnson

My advocacy began when my oldest son, Sean, was receiving physical, occupational and speech therapy. Sean had received these services starting at nine months old, as he was delayed in sitting up and all areas of development. His speech therapist had asked if I would be interested in assisting Easter Seals by collecting donations and speaking to local civic organizations. This would serve two purposes: helping Easter Seals and at the same time Easter Seals was helping us pay for Sean's speech therapy. At the time back in 1997, health insurance did not assist with speech therapy prior to age three.

Sean did not walk until he was 22 months old. He received his diagnosis of autism at age two. Once our family received the diagnosis, I attempted to educate myself on autism. The behavioral therapist who diagnosed my son gave me a book list on the topic of autism. I was a part time librarian at the time, so I requested most of the books through interlibrary loan. What I read did not seem to correlate with what I saw in my son. I sought another opinion from another evaluation team. They gave my son the diagnosis of pervasive development disorder.

At the time, that only delayed the inevitable, as I had to grow into acceptance of his diagnosis and learn more about autism.

Understand your child's needs. This was a rough concept for me. As I did not know what my son's needs most of the time were. He could not communicate his needs to me, as most of his verbal skills were repeating lines from tv shows and songs. Once my son started preschool at age three, I was worn out with the homework the speech therapist gave me, as I had parent expectations of my son choosing the right picture when I said ball. I was only to record the outcome of his homework and report back. I would continue to educate myself on autism, but there was so much I did not know. I understood my son's strengths and weaknesses. Identifying any barriers to his success was hard for me to recognize, I knew he needed help with potty training. I also knew that I needed help and at the time there were not that many resources. I depended on his school to fill those gaps.

Have a plan. It was to follow what my son's teacher would say at parent meetings and at our individual education plan meeting. I did want the teachers to work with my son and not to allow him to sit in the classroom and do nothing. I wanted the teacher and teacher assistants to challenge him, to get my son to try. In 2004, I had gotten a flyer in my son's backpack in regard to a family friendly zoo event sponsored by a local autism support group. Taking my son to such an event seemed risky to me at the time. I did not care to take my son much anywhere outside of family members' homes, church, and his school. I was concerned about how my son's behavior would be. This was an event for families that are affected by autism. I told myself that we needed to go.

The people at the zoo event were so welcoming and they also invited me to their support group meetings. I felt like a part of a new family. I felt accepted and understood. During the support group meetings, we could ask questions and get feedback. There was childcare for both my sons.

In 1999, my husband and I had another son. I was able to network and collaborate with other parents. At the time, I did not realize how important networking with other parents was. It was so vital to our success as parents, as a family and for my children. The other parents were my lifeline. I wanted to give to the group as much as they gave to me.

I felt so at home within the autism support group that within a year and with some encouragement from the other parent board members, I wanted to also be part of the parent board for the autism support group. I volunteered to return voicemails for our group. I helped with our group newsletter. I became involved with our fundraisers: our golf outing and our autism awareness walk. I brought my skills to help others and at the same time stretched myself beyond my comfort zone.

I received an abundant number of blessings from my involvement with the autism support group. One blessing was being introduced to the Prioritization of Urgency of Need for Services, PUNS. In the state of Illinois, where I live, the Division of Developmental Disabilities within the Department of Human Services, started the database in 2005 to begin collecting candidates and information for those to be eligible for services. At this time in my life, I was a single mom. I would struggle with trying to attend to all Sean's needs and help Sean's younger brother with homework. Home life in the evening, after work, was a juggling act. Within a few months I was notified by letter that Sean was awarded disability services through the state of Illinois. It was not until a year or more later that those services were put into place by way of respite care.

Respite care provides short-term relief for primary caregivers. As parents and special needs parents, we all need to take respite, a break. I started the hobby of scrapbooking in 2001, when invited to bring three photos to a gathering. Out of responsibility to make sure my photos were in an album that would not be compromised and would be protected for a lifetime, I found myself loving scrapbooking and crafting pages of my family photos. What I loved most about scrapbooking was the ability to get a break from my parental duties and to recharge, so when I did come home after my break, I was able to return without full burnout. Even if you are not a special needs parent, we all need to recharge.

Taking a break for me also benefitted both of my sons. If I was tired and stressed, I could not give my sons what they needed. If I did not allow myself time to recharge, I would not be able to be the best mother I could be for myself and my children. Taking a break from my children also allowed them the opportunity to get to see that mom is not always there and come to terms with mom being gone for a little bit. My children were also able to develop relationships with other family members and general caregivers. My youngest son learned to go to another adult other than mom when he needed help with a problem. In this way, we were able to develop problem solving skills by other means, that don't involve mom and dad.

While sometimes, you may not get a physical break from children, you can schedule breaks in your day. When Sean was taking a nap, I would watch my favorite television show or take a nap, too. I needed rest and I was not going to feel guilty about taking a nap. Sometimes household chores did not get done, but I did not get down about it. Our family had cooked meals, cleaned dishes and clothes, and everyone got their daily hygiene routine completed.

I am grateful for the services I received through PUNS. Before my son, Sean, aged out of high school, he was moved from the child developmental disability program to the adult developmental disability program. Sean could attend high school up to the age of 21 since he had a cognitive disability. Moving him to the adult developmental disability program allowed Sean to have day program services in place once he completed high school. Sean's cognitive ability did not allow him to live independently and the skills he acquired while in school could continue to be learned at the day program, so he did not lose those skills. Transitioning from the high school to the day program did take a period of adjustment for Sean. He did not care for change as is common with autism. After two years, Sean adjusted to the routine of going to the day program. I normally drop him off at the day program in the morning before going to work. He then would have a dedicated person that would pick him up in the afternoon and cared for him in the afternoon until I got home from work.

Another blessing I gained through the autism support group was the empowerment I received in learning to be an advocate for my autistic son. When our group hired an individual education program (IEP) coach, the Saturday morning training was free to parents. The coach handed out binders and handouts. I learned a brief overview of rights and special education law, the importance of written requests and documentation and how to generally prepare for the annual IEP meeting. I learned a lot that day. I loved how the parents would ask questions and we had genuine conversations about real-life situations.

When it came time to have our annual IEP meeting for Sean, I felt prepared after the training. I had done my homework. I was ready. Everyone at the IEP meeting signed the sign in sheet for attendance. Each member on the team gave their report of Sean's goals and accomplishments. I then shared my concerns. Each member of the team that could address my concerns spoke and gave feedback.

Then the lead of the special education team asked me a question. She said, "Ms. Paul, have all your concerns been addressed today?"

I smiled. I said, "Yes, they have."

When I left the meeting room, I had a feeling of triumph and success! I felt good for Sean. I felt good for me. I can do this!

As a result of that day, I felt encouraged to advocate for my son the rest of his 27 years of life and made it my mission to advocate for other parents as well.

Teresa D. Johnson

Teresa D. Johnson is an insurance professional, a blogger, author, and entrepreneur who resides in Taylorville, Illinois. Johnson was born in central Illinois and lived in Florida and Texas for a short time when she was young. It was during her time in Texas that she discovered her talent for writing and won first place in a statewide academic essay competition at the University of Texas in 1982. She later graduated with a Bachelor of Arts degree in journalism and political science. She freelanced for the Springfield Business Journal, a monthly business publication, from the fall of 2001 to January 2016.

Teresa is an anti-bully advocate supporting Stand for the Silent and a former six-year parent board member of the Autism Society of America Central Illinois Chapter. Teresa is a single parent and has advocated for both her sons: Sean and Nick. She advocated not only for autism, but ADHD in relation to her youngest son, Nick. From encouragement from her youngest son, she sought after an ADHD evaluation in November 2022 and was diagnosed with ADHD, December 2022.

Teresa has a passion to advocate for individuals with autism and their families by providing knowledge to access community services and financial solutions to help bring peace to the entire family.

Connect with Teresa at https://linktr.ee/officialtimewithteresa.

CHAPTER 19

First, Look in the Mirror, and Make a Change

Tiffiny Roper

I lost my dad over ten years ago, now. I was, and always will be, Daddy's girl. Though my dad did have some issues as a parent and made some unhealthy decisions, I always saw the intent behind the choices he made and judged his decisions more so than the outcome of those decisions. My dad was big on all his kids being leaders, not followers. He would even tell us if we were to get into trouble, he'd better not find out it was because we followed someone else and did what they said to do. Instead, we better have come up with the bad action ourselves. He would tell us that if we came up with the idea ourselves and got in trouble, we would be punished less.

When I was fifteen, I remember a specific trip I had with my grandma and one of her friend's granddaughters. I remember my grandma being particularly partial to this girl, so in order to be able to go talk to this cute guy we met on the beach (yes, fifteen, with all the boy-crazy hormones raging), I knew I would have to get her to ask my grandma so we could go meet them at the local store. After the trip, when my grandma told my parents what happened, my dad was angry that I was following this girl's ideas more than he was angry that we went away from our grandma to chat with this guy. I was quick to assure him, I didn't follow her ideas, I came up with the ideas myself. When he heard this, my punishment went down dramatically, just as my dad's anger about the overall situation. That lesson followed me throughout my life. It made me not take drugs when peer-pressured as a teen. It made me choose a lot of things in life that maybe I wouldn't have if I had been a follower. My dad raised me to be a confident leader, and I am grateful to him for that. I also watched as he role-modeled what a confident person looked like with the decisions he made in life. When my dad made a choice, it was black and white, good or bad, and he never looked back. He led with integrity, made what he felt was the only right decision, and moved on. I admired that quality in him, among others.

With my dad's role modeling and how he raised me, I have been confident in my decisions in life, starting at a pretty young age. I learned to follow my gut instincts, feeling someone's energy, and believing that feeling over the actions they took or the words they said. I also knew, at around eight years old, that I wanted to be a mom more than anything. So when my husband and I tried to get pregnant, after five years of marriage, I didn't know it was going to be so hard. After years of struggling, fertility treatments, and the horrendous loss of twins born alive early who lived for three and four hours and didn't survive, we were finally pregnant with two beautiful girls.

In going through everything I did just to have babies, I appreciated the experience of being a mom much more than maybe I would have. Early on, when the girls were only months old, I often found myself just trying to survive and I would *lie to myself* that I just needed to get through this *one* thing, then things would be fine. Whether it was the girls being sick or they were teething or my planning of their next birthday party, there was always the never-ending to do list. I quickly got caught up in trying to get everything done on that to do list and, at times, found, as they got older, I was putting the list first over having time with my girls. I eventually figured out I was living in *survival* mode by just trying to get through the next thing. I wasn't truly appreciating each moment and being present, as I should have. I decided to start reviewing what I really valued and reflected on what order my values should be in. Then I started organizing my life, and where I spent my time, based on that prioritized list of values. I quickly discovered how it made decision-making and prioritizing what was most important so much easier. For instance, if I valued love at the highest, then I would stop worrying about if the laundry was done and focus more on spending time with my kids and creating experiences and lifelong memories. This also made me get out of survival mode. I started looking around and realized many of my friends were living the same way, overwhelmed, and exhausted with too many things they were trying to get done at once. Now, I coach moms, helping them create their own list of goals and values and prioritize them to help create more confidence in themselves and, ultimately, give them the joy and fulfillment they truly want.

In order for us to raise confident kids, as parents, it starts with us, the beacons of light for our families. We cannot preach one thing to our kids and live another. Being a true leader first, as my dad was for me, and as I am for my girls, is so important. I enjoy raising confident, independent, loving girls that will be amazing leaders of tomorrow, and I started by being a confident role model, for them, with actions I take. One of the best ways to have confidence in yourself, as a parent, is to keep your word to yourself first. If you can't keep your word to yourself, you lose integrity with yourself and that lowers your own confidence. We often say, "I'll start the diet tomorrow" or any number of other goals that always start with *tomorrow* when we know we won't start them tomorrow. I also make sure to keep my word to my kids. If I say I am going to do something, I will try everything under the sun to make sure I get it done. It's important, when I make confident decisions, to show my kids integrity with myself, so they can believe what I say too. This really helps give them the structure in their life that they need to start building their own confidence.

Another way I work on confidence with my girls, just as I do with the parents I work with, is by having them set their own goals and work hard to achieve them. For instance, my girls are in Girl Scouts. During cookie season, I have them set high goals, not easy ones anybody can achieve. Then they set up a plan of what needs to be done in order for them to hit those goals.

I also make sure my girls are in several different types of activities, so they are always gaining different skills. In addition to Girls Scouts, my girls learn to be part of a team by playing softball. I also teach them leadership skills by placing them in positions like pitcher and catcher. Overall, I have taught them the importance of being a leader, not a follower, just as my Dad did for me. I have also taught them to make decisions based on their own thoughts behind their decisions, instead of following others, including what I think is best. If they have a good reason for why something should be done in a certain way, I listen and allow them to try. And if it doesn't work the first time, it's not failing but learning, adjusting, and trying again.

Another opportunity I had to help build confidence in my girls was by working with them in the kitchen when they were younger, as they love cooking and baking. They often talk about owning their own bakery and restaurant when they are older, and I love the idea of them owning their own future. A few months before they turned ten, they talked to me about trying to cook dinner on their own, without me standing there supervising. So, I nervously left the room and let them cook dinner completely by themselves. And the dinner turned out really good. They are now very confident cooks in the kitchen, after only a few months. People are often surprised what confident cooks they are and how good the food tastes.

Another thing I do, as their Mom, is I don't want to control my girls and tell them everything they need to do. I don't believe in yelling or threatening or punishing to scare my kids into doing things my way, or else. All this ends up doing, at the end of the day, is causing them to rebel as teens, just as I did. It's important, instead, that they understand the reasoning behind the choices I do make, so when they are older and I am not around, they can make confident, healthy decisions themselves. And when they do something wrong, instead of yelling or punishing, I talk to them and explain what was wrong with the action (and more importantly the thinking that got them to take that action), so they know why it might not work out well or as they had thought it would. Kids have to make their own mistakes, though we'd like to keep them from all the broken hearts and scrapes, or they won't be productive, healthy members of society and the leaders this world needs.

As parents, we must focus on self-care and loving ourselves, as we are, today - a human being who is always learning, a work in progress. If we are always stressed, and never happy, we role model that for our kids. Parents often forget the importance of giving grace to themselves, forgiving themselves for not being the perfect parent all the time, and of being kind and loving toward themselves. We are, instead, very critical of ourselves and, often times, the people around us. We should lift each other up, as we are not each other's competition. We need to look out for each other, and each other's children, like we are in a village with a large family. Also, if we don't have fulfillment and joy as parents in life, how can we ever expect our kids to? As we all see every day, they are only little for a little while, so just do your best to stay in the moment and be present with your kids. Focus on what's most important and be joyful, while regularly growing and learning, then role model that for our kids.

At the end of the day, parenting is hard. There isn't just one way to do things. And we live in scary times. Now, more so than maybe anytime in history, we need kids that are confident, so they are confident leaders this world needs for tomorrow. Keeping your word to yourself and your kids, having them set high goals for themselves, enrolling them in several activities so they can learn different skills, giving your kids the opportunity to make their own mistakes while helping them understand the reasoning behind decisions we make, teaching them the importance of being a leader instead of a follower, and first starting with ourselves as confident leaders (who are working on our own goals and role modeling the struggles and the successes to our children), will give your kids the confidence they need, today and tomorrow, and to also be confident parents to their own kids (your grandkids) one day. After all, if you want to make the world a better place, you have to first look at yourself and make a change.

Tiffiny Roper

Tiffiny Roper is on a mission to create amazing female leaders of tomorrow that this world desperately needs. She accomplishes this as a Life Coach for Moms of young daughters, working passionately with them to reach their goals and becoming the best role models they can be. In doing so, they live with a new purpose-driven life filled with joy and inspire those around them to do the same, starting with their daughters. She uses her twenty years of Project Management experience to keep Moms accountable in hitting their goals. She's also a speaker and best-selling author that loves creating memories with her husband of twenty years and young twin daughters, Avery and Sophia, including coaching their softball team and leading their Girl Scout troop.

Connect with Tiffiny at

https://www.facebook.com/groups/girlmomcoaching.

CHAPTER 20

The Parent I Choose to Be

Vera Thomas

Parenting is not an easy thing to do.
It takes courage, patience, and lots of prayer too.
Having a child changes a life.
Our goal should be lifting them to higher heights.
Children see what we do
And hear what we say.
Sometimes our own issues
Can get in the way.
We have no control
how we might have been raised.
Good, bad, or indifferent
We can choose better ways.
To develop our children to be their best
We may need to acknowledge and confess

That there are things we may need to learn.
Allowing some attitudes and behaviors
To crash and burn.
We cannot teach what we do not know.
Seeking wisdom and guidance
So, we and our children can grow
Into what God intended us to be.
It all begins at home.
And may improve our society.

I knew there had to be a better way. Having grown up with no confidence or self-esteem, as a result of negative taunts from both peers and adults. As a child, I would often cry and pray asking God, "Why was I born? What is my purpose?"

In my early teens, I was introduced to a book called the *Magic of Believing*, by Claude Bristol. The book changed my life. One of the quotes in the book:

No one can make you feel inferior without your permission.
~ Eleanor Roosevelt

That really resonated with me. I began to realize that it did not matter what other people said about me or how other people felt about me, what mattered was what I said to myself and how I felt about me. Through the continuation of reading self-help books and practicing what I read, I became confident, secure, and self-assured.

In my mid-20s, I found that my passion and my purpose was to make a difference in the lives of other people through training programs and public speaking. Also, during that time, I had a lot of female problems and three doctors told me I would never have children. The last doctor that I saw said with corrective surgery a child was possible. He suggested that I come back after I got married. Marriage was not in the cards at that point in time, so I put this on the back burner.

Life was going great! I was doing training programs and speaking. I had gotten a contract to provide training for adults. I also provided training for different youth programs. When I did get married, the trajectory of my life changed. I went back to the doctor that had told me I needed the surgery in order to conceive. I had the surgery and became pregnant a year after I was married. During my three-year marriage, I was mentally, physically, and emotionally abused resulting in the miscarriage of my first child. A year later I became pregnant again. My baby's due date was the same date as the child I lost.

When my son was three months old, my ex-husband attacked me in front of him. I realized at that point; I did not want to raise a child in that kind of environment. I left for a couple of months and stayed with a friend. I came back and prepared to leave permanently. I raised my son as a single mother from the time he was six months old.

All the confidence and self-esteem I had worked so hard to acquire was gone. Because of the abuse, I found it very difficult to continue working with others to build their confidence and self-esteem. As a result, I no longer felt authentic in doing the work, so I discontinued that kind of work.

I had to start all over rebuilding and regaining my confidence and self-esteem. This time, I was not only doing it for myself; I had a child. I knew that I did not want my child to ever feel like I felt growing up, belittled, ridiculed, called names, or told, "You are nothing, you will never be anything." I vowed to never do that to my son. I never did. Do not get it twisted, the times when he did things that could have been addressed by name calling, I learned to address the behavior and not attack him as a person. I might say something like, "That was a stupid thing that you did." I would add, "I'm not calling you stupid, you are better than this behavior!" "Help me understand why you did this." My son is one of the most positive, confident, and self-assured people you will ever meet.

There are other attitudes and behaviors that we may have experienced as a child that we do not need to impose upon our children. I want to take some time to address those things that are considered misconceived behaviors, that we bring into parenting because of our own experiences. While there are at least 20 of these behaviors that were identified in an article I read a few years ago, I will address a few. Upon reading the article and doing research, I developed a tool for parents to assess and identify any behaviors they may be displaying.

Making Character Attacks - Take a negative action from others and blow it up into a personality flaw resulting in belittling, criticizing, demeaning, or intentionally saying things that are hurtful out of frustration or anger. Perhaps doing so in front of others. People may do this with their children by calling them lazy, bad or by comparing them to their other siblings. This is also done when someone is upset or angry with their significant other.

Causes for this behavior – I am sure you have heard, "Hurt people, hurt people." Someone may have grown up being treated this way or may have experienced it as an adult themselves. It is a defense mechanism when feeling threatened by what is being said. Even if the statement is true and based on facts and evidence.

Impact of this behavior on a child or anyone:

- Feelings of helplessness.
- Lack of confidence.

- Low self-esteem.
- Poor performance.
- May cause irreparable damage to a child.
- Could ruin the reputation or credibility of an adult.
- Persistent depressed mood.
- Anxiety.
- Irritability.
- Sleep problems.
- Eating disorders.

Alternatives:

- Acknowledge their positive attributes. Let our children know their positive qualities, attitude, and behaviors.
- Address the behavior with facts and evidence.
- Ask questions to process the behavior.
- Help them identify positive options to replace the behavior.
- Set boundaries - not accepting any type of personal attack.
- Do not allow siblings to character attack each other.

If your child is being bullied in this manner emphasize:

No one can make you feel inferior without your permission.
~ Eleanor Roosevelt

Using this quote while giving them time and letting them speak positive affirmations about themselves will serve as a buffer against such attacks.

Avoiding Conflict Altogether - Rather than discussing frustration in a calm, respectful manner, we may not say anything or are ready to explode and then blurt it out in an angry, hurtful way. We may experience physical/health issues from keeping thoughts and feelings inside.

Causes for this behavior - Afraid of getting hurt or being rejected. May feel uncomfortable perhaps due to having experienced character attacks when expressing in the past. To avoid a power struggle, choose not to say anything. May have a passive/aggressive personality with a tendency to keep things held in until reaching a boiling point.

Behavior Indications

- Withdrawal from conflict when it arises.
- Unexpressed anger or resentment.
- Assumptions and expectations vs. communications.
- Not speaking up for self.
- Efforts to please the other person.
- You excessively apologize.
- Resentment.
- Frustration.
- Contempt.
- Breakdown in communications.

Alternatives

- Talk about conflict early and often. Do not hold things inside. If it is a difficult or touchy subject, acknowledge that it is by starting the conversation with something like, "This is uncomfortable for me however, it needs to be discussed." Be respectful of the other person.

- Agree to disagree.
- Mutually agreed upon solutions.
- Take a break to cool off and talk later.
- Be willing to hear the other person out.
- Stay calm, and do not get defensive.

Being Defensive - Rather than addressing complaints with an objective eye and willingness to understand the other person's point of view there is denial of any wrongdoing or acceptance of the possibility of being a contributor to the problem or issue.

Denying responsibility may seem to alleviate stress in the short run, however, creates long-term problems when family members do not feel listened to and unresolved conflicts continue to grow.

Causes for this behavior

- Trauma or abuse in childhood makes a person crave power.
- Anxiety or depression.
- Lack of confidence or self-esteem
- Reaction to conceal the truth.
- Reaction to feeling helpless.
- Response to shame or guilt.
- Learned behavior from others.

Behavior Indications

- Stops listening to the other person completely.

- Justifies actions.
- Accuses someone else of making the mistake.
- Blames another person.
- Makes excuses.
- Bring up past instances rather than talking about the present situation.

Impact of this behavior - Defensive behaviors can distract from feelings, particularly.

- Feelings of shame or hurt. The core purpose of defensiveness is to turn the attention away.
- From self and toward the faults of the other person. In this way, we are directing blame.
- Toward the other person. Children learn to do the same when they see it in their parents.

Alternatives

- Listen before rushing to defend self.
- Seek clarification to understand the accusation.
- Take responsibility – Own up – See as opportunity.
- Ask how you can improve the situation.
- Fix the problem.
- Teach children to do the same.

The Blame Game - Not accepting responsibility for our choices. Blaming everything and everybody for things being the way they are.

After I left my husband, I was bitter. I remember a friend stopping by my house. I started in with "If it wasn't for him, my life would not be this way!" She looked me in my eyes and said, "No Vera, if it wasn't for you and the choices you have made, your life would not be this way!" Of course, that did not go over very well with me. I thought, "How dare she blame me for my situation!" The truth of the matter is that accepting responsibility for our choices can be a hard pill to swallow. It is one that needs to be swallowed. Once I realized she was correct. Had I not married him, (which there were warning signs that I did not take heed), my life would have been totally different. The positive consequence of that choice was my son. Had I not gotten married, I most likely would not have my son.

Once I started accepting responsibility and the consequences for my choices, I was able to convey how important it is to my son.

Causes for this behavior - It is all about perception. "How will I be perceived if I take ownership for my behaviors and actions."

Behavior Indications

- Finger-pointing: People may point fingers at others.
- Denial: People may deny their responsibility.
- Exclusion: People may consistently exclude or marginalize a member of the group, and then make them the scapegoat when things go wrong.

Impact of this behavior - It impacts our relationship with our children and also teaches our children to play the blame game.

Alternatives

- As a parent – Model accepting responsibility.
- Teach kids to take ownership.
- Discuss choices and consequences.
- "It's not my fault" is not an option.

- Ask questions.
- As a result of accepting responsibility and the consequences for my choices, I was able to model and teach my son to do the same. That is one of the things I value and appreciate about him.

Conclusion

Awareness precedes change. When we know better, we do better. I encourage parents to assess the misconceived behaviors they may have learned from their childhood or from others and explore alternatives. Remember, our children grow to be what they see!

Vera Thomas

Vera Thomas is a Certified Life Coach, Speaker, Trainer, Mediator, and Poet 20x Best Selling Author, Producer of a weekly podcast/radio show "The Vera Thomas Show." Her show is on Tuesdays and Thursday at 7pm EST.

It is her goal to help others overcome circumstances that diminish and help them to surge ahead with their dreams. Vera, against all odds, completed a degree in psychology from Walsh University in Canton, OH. She graduated *Cum Laude* She also has a master's degree.

Vera has worked with companies, organizations, schools, churches, and non-profits developing, designing, and delivering soft skills training and leadership programs. Being a poet, she developed an after-school program allowing students to express themselves through poetry, short stories, songs or rap. She teaches presentation skills and vision boards. Other programs for youth include an all-school assembly "I Believe in Me," an anti-bully program called "Using My Power," and "My Greatness" is designed to increase self-esteem and confidence.

As a result of her work with children who shared about their home environments, Vera developed a program for parents, "Instilling

Greatness in Myself and My Children" - Parents examine attitudes and behaviors that impact their children's lives. Vera is available for companies who want to transform their teams or families who want to transform their lives.

As a Certified Coach, Vera works with families, children and individuals. She is available as a speaker.

Connect with Vera at https://bit.ly/VeraThomas.

the

LANGUAGE OF PLAY

with

DINALYNN ROSENBUSH, SLP

HELPING KIDS LISTEN BETTER WITH CONNECTION AND COMMUNICATION STRATEGIES

is an Educator and veteran Speech Language Pathologist of 25+ years, Author, Speaker, and Host of the podcast, The Language of Play, which is ranked Top 2% Globally in the categories of "Parenting" and "Kids and Family." Her most significant title is Mother and Grandmother.

After many years being asked, "Why Won't Kids Listen?," Dinalynn wrote a Coaching Program that answers that question, and to help parents gain skills to connect in ways their child's brain understands. Currently, she Is a Speaker, Consultant, and Parenting Coach sharing skills and strategies to better communicate and connect with kids. She teaches parents how to expand their child's speech and language skills - whether the child has speech and language delays, is a dual-language learner, or is developing normally.

Her solid foundation comes from her work with hundreds of students and their parents, which resulted not only in better skills for the students, but also in better family relationships. Her mission is to help families build happier, more productive, heart-centered homes through good communication and strong, loving connection. Dinalynn enjoys speaking for Schools, Churches, and Parent Groups educating parents on HOW we teach language.

She raised her children as a creative, adventure loving, single parent that knows the importance of working together, as a TEAM, for the family system to function well.

Connect with Dinalynn at
www.DinalynnRosenbush.com

About the Producer

JACI FINNEMAN is the founder and parenting coach of Hello World, LLC & No-Problem Parenting™. She is committed to helping parents become confident leaders for their children, along with finding happiness in their day-to-day routines and bringing peace back into their homes. For more than 30 years, Jaci has worked as a Family Counselor turned Parent Coach, meeting with kids and parents directly in their homes (in person or virtually) and helping them to deal with and overcome their emotional and behavioral challenges.

In 2013, Jaci started Hello World, a company dedicated to empowering parents to become the confident leaders their kids crave them to be through a model she calls No-Problem Parenting™. Making an intentional shift in teaching kids and parents how to give "the problem" less attention and instead, focus on the solution.

As a Parent-Coach, Parenting Strategist, Speaker and Leader, Jaci has more than 50,000 hours of experience working with parents and children affected by trauma and mental health diagnosis. Her down-to-earth, authentic and relatable personality adds light, hope, and clarity to her clients. One of 100 first cousins, she enjoys all things baseball, hockey, and dirt. She and her husband of 27 years live in Central Minnesota with their teenage son.

Acknowledgments

Thank you, Kohila Silvas, for introducing me to Action Takers Publishing for Volume Two of No-Problem Parenting™.

Lynda Sunshine-West, I want to express my sincere gratitude to you. You are truly an exceptional person who inspires and motivates others to make a positive impact in the world. Your unwavering dedication to your purpose and drive is truly inspiring. I appreciate you and Sally Green so much for your guidance and support as we collaborated on this book.

Thank you to the authors who have generously shared their experiences and insights in this book. Your passion and dedication to empowering parents and their children are truly commendable and invaluable. Your stories have not only inspired but also equipped readers with essential knowledge and skills to navigate the challenges of raising a family in today's world. I am honored to be connected with you;

Vera Thomas, Tiffiny Roper, Teresa Dawn Johnson, Ruthanne Warnick, Rosalind Sedacca, Dr. Mort Orman, Mardi Winder-Adams, Kohila Sivas, Kimberly Gawne, Khrystyna Chorna, Kelly Flood, Dr. Kate Lund, Julie Kenzler, Joy Bartholomew, Dr. JJ Kelly, Helen Snell, Elvira Di'Brigit, Denise and Victoria Schwendeman, Dr. Christy Matusiak, I am grateful for each of you.

To my father-in-law, Nicholas Finneman. I want to express my heartfelt gratitude for your unwavering support and inspiration during my entrepreneurial journey over the past decade. Our conversations have been incredibly valuable, and I have learned so much from the stories and experiences you've shared about your own journey as an entrepreneur. Your dedication to helping others is truly inspiring, and your role as a grandfather is exceptional - our family cherishes the love you show us. Thank You, I love and respect you very much.

Jaci Finneman

Printed by Libri Plureos GmbH in Hamburg,
Germany